INFLUENCER NETWORKING SECRETS

ENDORSEMENT PAGE

"If you want the opportunities and recommendations that always seem to go to one person in the room, read *Influencer Networking Secrets*. These principles will help you pick the locks on a lot of barriers, especially if you're just starting out."

- Vince Del Monte,
Bestselling Author,
http://www.GetLivingLarge.com

"If you've ever wanted to become the 'invisible man' who walks right through walls and past gatekeepers, read *Influencer Networking Secrets*. This is the performance-driven guide to create powerful business relationships."

- David L. Hancock,
Wall Street Journal Bestselling Author
of *Performance Driven Thinking*

"I know how powerfully these principles change lives around the world. If you want to make deep personal impact and end up in rooms you have no business being in, *Influencer Networking Secrets* will teach you how to walk right past the competition, the gatekeepers and the conventional wisdom."

- Aaron Walker,
Founder and President, *View From the Top*

"Relationships are the currency of every age - but particularly this one. The greater caliber your relationships have, the more you'll succeed and influence people in every way - from opportunities to dating to health. *Influencer Networking Secrets* teaches you to build a strong, diverse network that gives you inroads to power and influence."

- Adam Connors,
Founder, *NetWorkWise.com*

"I have literally done exactly what Paul teaches, in terms of becoming a Pro Bono Publicist. The strategies in this book will skyrocket your reputation and recognition in your industry. *Influencer Networking Secrets* is essential reading."

- Giuseppe Grammatico,
Host, *Franchise Freedom*

"Relationships are the most valuable asset we possess in business. Influencer Networking Secrets will teach you how to plant, nurture and harvest a fortune in relationship capital."

- **Kevin Thompson**,
Founder, *Tribe For Leaders*

"By boldly brandishing the banner of faith in the arena of wealth creation, my friend, the respected business professional Paul Edwards reveals the relational road map to real riches. Every page of this incandescent book carries compelling insights that demonstrate how to maximize time and leverage effort to bring fiscal transformation to every reader. Bring your own courage and determination, and this book will supply all else."

- **Rabbi Daniel Lapin**,
Radio & Television Personality,
Author of *Thou Shall Prosper*

INFLUENCER NETWORKING SECRETS

How to Build the Magnetic Influence,
Meaningful Connection and Profitable Publicity
of a Radically Generous Entrepreneur

PAUL S. EDWARDS

NEW YORK

LONDON • NASHVILLE • MELBOURNE • VANCOUVER

Influencer Networking Secrets

How to Build Magnetic Influence, Meaningful Connection and
Profitable Publicity of a Radically Generous Entrepreneur

Published in New York, New York, by Morgan James Publishing. Morgan James is a
trademark of Morgan James, LLC. www.MorganJamesPublishing.com

ISBN 9781631952524 paperback
ISBN 9781631952531 eBook
Library of Congress Control Number: 2020939911

Cover Design by:
Megan Dillon
megan@creativeninjadesigns.com

Interior Design by:
Christopher Kirk
www.GFSstudio.com

Morgan James is a proud partner of Habitat for Humanity Peninsula
and Greater Williamsburg. Partners in building since 2006.

Get involved today! Visit
MorganJamesPublishing.com/giving-back

"...to the service of that great and glorious Being, who is the beneficent Author of all the good that was, that is or that will be..." - George Washington

TABLE OF CONTENTS

Foreword xv
Preface – Influencer Networking Secrets xix
Acknowledgments xxxiii

Chapter 1 - My Beginnings: From Awkward, Pushy
        Salesman to Radically Generous
        Entrepreneur 1

The #1 lesson learned selling insurance; how master-minds and coaching changed the game; how I profited from participating with nonprofits; the monetary reward of being an evangelist and an educator; the magnetic power of monasticism; pulling profit from free publicity for others; making dreams come true by networking with dream connections; piercing and persuading with print; the cure of curating your tribe

Chapter 2 – The Monastic Heart
        (Be a Magnet, Not a Pusher). 23

Pushers versus Magnets; how to get people to talk about insurance; the 3 pillars of personal magnetism; the importance of polarity

Chapter 3 – Golden (Pro Bono Publicity) 41

The least expensive, most powerful form of advertising; the least-downloaded podcast EVERYONE wants to be on; practical ways to publicize your network; the right time to do paid advertising; how to provide publicity for people who already have plenty of it

Chapter 4 – The Inroads
        (Not-For-Profit IS For-Profit) 59

What NOT to do when you serve in a nonprofit; the centrality of clear vision and proper motives; the ravenous appetite of the 501(c)3 marketplace for entrepreneurial leadership; how "dirty work" yields the spoils of nonprofit leadership; basic nonprofit leadership mentality

Chapter 5 – Owning It (How to Network
        with Dream Connections). 79

How to make an executive into an ally in thirty seconds or less; becoming an "angler" who can catch the big fish; keeping your ear to the ground for things influencers miss; pre-assembled publicity packages to make a public figure smile; the 3 big questions that work in your house and the White House; the power of 1,000 reps on the "farm team" to score a hit with ONE key figure

Chapter 6 – Frequency (Persuasion in Print) 97

A more-than-three-sentence e-mail that almost ANY entrepreneur will read; putting a "heat signature" on your messages; when to speak, and when to communicate in print; how I made a micromanager happy on e-mail; how to think like a journalist and write like a copywriter; the memorability and brand power of "mechanisms"; how to deal with a printed "no"

Chapter 7 – The Curator
    (Focusing on the Outcome) 121

The downside of democratization for the entrepreneur; how to curate your outbound relationship building; how to define your client avatar; the duality of "curating yourself"; curating what goes into your heart, mind and soul; how to use polarity to curate your audience; how to curate prospects and clients; the outcomes we choose

Let's Work Together 141
About The Author 143

FOREWORD

August 20, 2017. Maybe it wasn't a red-letter day for you, but it was for me. And for Paul.

At the foothills of the mountains in Colorado, surrounded by breathtaking beauty and like-minded allies, our lives changed. I was there when everything changed for Paul. A lot of things changed for many of us that day. Ripples still radiate through my heart and mind from that weekend. I believe they will continue, until I breathe my last.

Disruption. Adventure. Change. Life. Abandonment of any semblance of a "comfort zone." Advancing into new territory. A turning point — perhaps, *the* turning point — for Paul.

I was there. I have been there ever since, walking

through life with Paul over these last few years as he's navigated through massive decisions and profound circumstances. I'm grateful and deeply honored to do so.

I've seen the lessons he's learned play out in real-time.

I've been a sounding board to man seeking to serve and inspire others.

I'm an ally in the corner of a warrior, seeking to bring honor to the Creator.

I'm honored to be counted among Paul's closest confidants.

I'm proud of all he's done. I'm excited about all that's still to come.

Over the last decade, I've averaged reading at least one book a month. I've yet to come across a complete, comprehensive book on any given subject. This book is not that, nor is it designed to be. *Influencer Networking Secrets* provides a real-world framework for increasing your influence and reach. This book is much more about *how to be* versus *what to do*.

You will learn from a practitioner. Paul does not approach his work academically — he invites you into his life. He shares real things, from a life examined, that serve to advance — from both failure and success. His actions *are* his words. His story impacts yours.

As you read, turn inward. Take time and apply these things to your own life, circumstances and aspirations. Visualize yourself in the text. Apply the nuggets of wisdom you find in these pages, and watch the trajectory of your life transform.

I've watched Paul's life evolve, using these principles. I hope the same comes true for you.

More importantly, I hope you hear the compassion, grace and love of the divine Creator in the echoes of what you read. It is what transforms and guides him, and me. It will do no less for you.

May your talents and abilities improve the lives of others.

May your joy abound.

Dave Culbreath

PREFACE

Who Are You?

I'll start with this: "It's a privilege to be much clearer on that question."

The truth is, for many years I was considerably less certain. I could tell you who I was in relation to others. I could tell you who I dreamed of becoming. I was ready and willing to share my past. But the present was still shrouded in uncertainty.

The difference with this, the third version of my book, is proof of concept. I wrote the 2018 and 2019 versions in a "prophetic" posture. They were published and released before I really had something to show for the content. I'm fond of quoting Denholm Elliott, in the movie "Indiana Jones and the Last Crusade": I knew "everything, except where to begin."

My name is no more or less significant than the next author you'll read. This isn't a book about *personalities*. It's about becoming a <u>certain kind of person</u>. Perhaps even a manifesto, if you will, about becoming the kind of person who moves throughout the world in a manner profoundly different from the pack. A man who walks right through barriers others think are impossible.

The Book of Proverbs uses the lizard to characterize a person who can "be caught with the hand, yet lives in kings' palaces." I don't know many people eager to be compared with the creature itself, but I like the spiritual meaning. What I teach and model in this book gets exemplified by those vulnerable yet cunning little reptiles. They're content to sit in the shadows, camouflaged by their environment, for lengthy periods. In fact, it's the only way they survive. A lizard in constant motion is usually avoiding a predator.

Lizards excel at adapting to their environment. They can live rent-free in mansions if that's their nearest shelter. You'll observe this in the stories I share. I kept getting invited into rooms and circles for which I was clearly unqualified. I hobnobbed casually with people others were afraid to approach. It's been an incredible ride.

So no matter what work butters my bread, the first card I flash is that of a highly relational person and professional. It is a cornerstone value in my life — deep and meaningful connection with God and other human beings. I'm lost without it.

Okay, fine. But what do you do?

Another question I'm grateful to answer more definitively.

Occupationally, the best way to put it is "executive ghostwriter." I employ my talent as a voice mimic and skills as a writer. I mix it with experience-building influence and everything I've learned through coaching and masterminds. I create "plug-and-play":

Blogs

Micro-content

E-mails

Audio/video scripts

Audio/video show notes and descriptions

Sales pages/letters

Expert non-fiction books

Sales funnel buildout copy

I serve mainly faith-based influencers, coaches and consultants. My work, simply put, is to *become you on paper*.

If you've read the 2019 version of this book, you may remember the difference. I dreamed (and still dream) of creating my own mastermind group. I mentor younger generations through the church I attend. My dream is to create a mentoring mastermind network for young men in the Judeo-Christian tradition, particularly in the ever-expanding world of technology. The time for that will soon arrive.

Beyond that comes all of my experience as an influencer myself. I also facilitate strategic connections. My friend and mentor Kevin Thompson helped me put words to this. (Okay, actually, I stole it from him. He's currently considering suing me for the rights!) It goes, "I connect executives and entrepreneurs with pre-qualified partners and prospects who want to talk about working together."

To compound awkward animal comparisons, Jesus told us to "be wise as serpents and harmless as doves." Neither creature would probably win the meme contest on social media. We love to see ourselves represented by regal-looking lions or fierce wolves. Not many of us want a venomous viper or a dopey bird that flutters and coos.

That aside, I think the genius of this statement is overlooked. Dallas Willard commented on the "wise as serpents" piece by describing how serpents stalk their prey. They do not attack head-on, tackling like a lion. They don't roar and snarl. They watch and observe, waiting until the time is right. But when they move, they do so decisively.

The only problem is that snakes can't see worth a lick.

Stay with me on this! This is relevant to what I do. More importantly, it's relevant to _how I do it,_ which makes all the difference.

When I was 16, I owned a ball python as a pet. Snakes fascinated me at the time. I watched documentaries and read books on them. And one thing I remember is that snakes actually have poor vision. If you were to stand a field mouse next to a grey-colored rock of similar size, the snake could not <u>visually</u> tell the difference.

Instead, these creatures sense their prey through tiny infrared sensors built into their upper lip, called *thermo-receptors*. To me, this means that when Jesus said, "Be wise as serpents," he wasn't referring to gauging a situation through your eyes. He meant that you measure the <u>heat signature, or, in other words, the temperature of an interaction of exchange</u>.

Watch for tension, defensiveness, warmth or people telling you what they think you want to hear. Don't listen just to what they say; watch what they <u>do</u>. Behavior, as Willard also said, will disclose to you what people truly believe, 100 percent of the time.

If you've ever "cold-called" someone in sales, you know what it means to have a "Minnesota in January" conversation. Likewise for people head over heels in love. You know what country singer Jake Owen meant when he sang, "It's a hundred-and-three between her and me, and only ninety-two in Daytona." There are audible, visible and behavioral dimensions to all of this. Together, they form the "heat signature" of connection.

If I've become more adept at anything over the years, it's sensing the heat signature between people. I do this both in conversations where I'm a participant, and in ones I overhear. I am much more attuned to *how* people give and receive communication. I care more than the average person about how things are said, and how they're received.

Other Duties

Having a good sense of a heat signature doesn't cancel out other biblical wisdom that guides my responses, either. "There is a time to be silent and a time to speak," warns Ecclesiastes. I exhibit this by standing alone, contentedly, in the lobby of the church we attend between services. Dozens of people pass me in either direction. They pay no attention to me. People I want to talk to pass by, and I practice restraining myself from moving toward them. I have learned that benevolence and compassion don't always translate into pursuing people.

Another interesting facet of this is how people often turn to me as a counselor. I have no degrees or qualifications in psychology. I've always been curious about what makes people tick. But I've learned the discipline of having that fascination without making a big deal of it. I know how to listen to people's disclosures without rushing to judgment or tips and techniques. Our deepest longings go much further than quick fixes. We want to be known and loved for who we are. The salesperson or copywriter who can do this shall inherit the earth.

Okay, that's cool. A good writer needs a good book. Why the emphasis on relationships?

Nothing I've achieved has happened apart from relationships. There have got to be many people like me strewn across the globe. Gifted wordsmiths with a global background and a bodybuilding habit. Verbally talented men and women who can project someone else's personality and voice onto paper. But the way things changed for me in the last 12 months only came about for one reason. I know how to get in the good graces of the right people. And I keep doing it until it works.

You'll notice that every chapter in this book deals with two key ingredients: you and other people. How you should engage them. How to communicate with them. How to choose them. How to get their attention in 60 seconds. There isn't much to say about your individual talent; I don't care what it is. It's good, it's important … but if talent was all it took, then everyone could succeed at something.

Grant Cardone pointed this out when he observed that most of the products and services we're aware of are NOT the best ones. The brand names that dominate the landscape and make fortunes in sales are the ones most skilled at *marketing*. And by the word "marketing," don't jump to paid advertising concepts like billboards or radio ads. Think more along the lines of "persuasion," "branding" and "building connection."

In 2020, this is still done best through face-to-face interaction. But a powerful secondary to that is the digital presence we have through social networks and content sharing, particularly in the wake of the coronavirus scare. I have become very adept at what I call "worming," as in "worming my way into people's consciousness." I use both real-life and digital connections with people to build a narrative. This gives me a chance to "bypass" the rat race of paid ads and nonstop digital noise to create top-of-mind awareness.

The work of relationships is never over, either. Even though I've struck oil, I'm profoundly aware of the need to continue building. In the Gospel of Luke, Jesus tells the disciples, "Use worldly wealth to gain friends for yourselves, so that when it's gone you will be welcomed into eternal dwellings." Personal connections are subject to the laws of entropy and motion. Add value for someone you know, and you enhance the likelihood of reciprocity. Neglect your connections, and they'll soon fade out of view. When the day comes that you need them, they'll be nowhere to be found.

That's why, to this day, I seek to embody and point people toward the lifestyle of the Radically Generous Entrepreneur. The longer I've had to think about this, the more I've found words to summarize it.

Radically Generous Entrepreneur - Someone so skilled in their work, it's a mystery how deftly they handle people.

I tried previously to describe the Radically Generous Entrepreneur as a client avatar. I see now that it's quite vague. The concept is much more apt as an aspirational identity. Something people can grow into, but that is not necessarily descriptive of their current status.

Nevertheless, the practices and philosophy you'll read in this book will get you there. I say this because I've lived it on and off for the last 20 years. For me, it operated the same way success in business does. You have a long season of "pushing" to make things happen, like pushing a bicycle up a steep hill. Then, when you reach the summit, the wheels begin to roll on their own and gather speed and momentum that's difficult to stop.

So, if you want to become a Radically Generous Entrepreneur, this book will be a constant guide. These strategies have worked for me everywhere and "every-when" I've tried them. They worked in British telephone customer service. They worked in the deserts of Iraq, among U.S. soldiers. They work on left-of-center college campuses and right-wing radio talk shows. They work for financial professionals and specialty trade contractors. They work in your own backyard, and they work around the world. They work for people of all faiths, including secular humanists.

These principles are based in timeless, unchanging truths about the human experience. The <u>delivery</u> method might change. The givers and receivers remain as human as can be. People may no longer show up to local networking groups. It doesn't mean they don't want to network! It's just that the things that <u>do</u> change, like technology, force us to become a lot smarter about <u>how</u> and <u>with whom</u> we network. The Radically Generous Entrepreneur's response and responsibility here doesn't change, either. Adapt. Connect. Give. Repeat.

Why did you write this book?

I've always wanted to answer this the way actor George Clooney described accepting his first major roles: *"I accepted my publishing deal ... because it was offered to me.*" (I appreciate you putting up with my attempts at humor.)

Think about it, now ... how do you get a major publishing house to even acknowledge your existence as a human being, let alone read your book, or offer to publish it? Why, I know the answer! It's through the power of relationships, of course. (Or do you still think I mailed in a manuscript and just "got lucky"?)

Of course, there's one reason that hasn't changed: I'd like to make a living. I might single-handedly be keeping the local GNC store in business with my supplement habit. If you like how I write and would be willing to trade your hard-earned dollars, I'm always open to conversations. That way, I can still afford my next plastic containers full of electrolyte and BCAA drink mixes.

A second reason is a personal one. I'd like to have a version of this book that supersedes the first. Have you ever looked at a creative endeavor you did several years earlier and shuddered? There are things in "Business Beyond Business" I'm happy to exclude from this version.

What were NOT among the reasons you wrote this book?

Part of influencer life involves realizing not everyone's cut out for the same lifestyle. Circumstances prevent it. Some settle for work that doesn't require a whole lot of skill with people. Others work in fields that do, but they can't afford to hire a full-time writer. I'm not expecting this book to become a blockbuster. I just want the right people to read it.

All that is to say that I want to reach a narrow audience: Kingdom-oriented thought leaders, influencers and coaches/consultants who don't have the bandwidth to maintain a steady stream of written content.

Secondly, I just want to build connections with people. Who's offended if you don't need my services? Certainly not me. It'd just be good for us to know each other if you read this and it resonates. You know people I'd like to meet, and vice versa. This book is all about who knows you, who has felt your impact and really wants to know more and return the favor.

So as much as I might need to earn a living, I'm all the more obsessed with helping others succeed. Reliably, this is how I find God bending his ear toward security and prosperity for my family. Be obsessed with helping His other children get theirs. He'll take care of yours.

This is a key affirmation I learned from my friend, Rabbi Daniel Lapin. Daily, when I awake, I thank God for the privilege of serving Him … by serving His other children. As a father of two young boys, nothing gives me greater pleasure than to see my sons cooperate on something productive. Teamwork between brothers dwelling in unity commands the Lord's blessing.

This book is a fundamental, unequivocal rejection of

get-rich-quick schemes and short-term strategies. Nothing you are about to learn will resuscitate your business if it's on life support. You will not make a million dollars overnight. In fact, this reminds me of a great quote from my friend Larry McNair. I encourage you, "If you want to make a million dollars, provide a million dollars' worth of service." And do it long before you actually get paid. As in months, years or even decades before you command it.

I worship a God who decrees times and seasons for everything. Dwelling outside time, this God is not rushed or anxious. He's not put off by long waits, and he can outlast anyone. I have been trained in this over 20 years of professional chaos and futility. When I began, I was over-delivering like crazy ... working in a call center! In the interim, as a soldier and then as an insurance salesman, I over-delivered like crazy. Now, nearing age 40, I'm also over-delivering like crazy doing something I'd only dreamed I could do for a living. It takes a lot of maturity and pursuit of true humility to be positioned for what God now gives me to do.

Many things were foggy to me in 2018 and 2019 when I wrote "10 Secrets to Networking Success" and "Business Beyond Business." I didn't know who I now know. I didn't know what I didn't know. But for what it's worth, I stand by what I wrote in both books. It was all part of a learning experience that's led me where I am today. I still use today what I wrote about using then. I hope that in reading this, you will find a piece of eternity you can cling to as a business professional. And I certainly hope we can connect!

With Love and Honor,

Paul

ACKNOWLEDGMENTS

Relationships take years, sometimes decades, to cultivate. I have a long list of people to thank, made longer by the enormous growth and change I underwent through the editions of this book. It's not September 2018 anymore.

Way back when, it was my dad, Tony Edwards, who first taught me to use word processing software. A gifted writer himself, he modeled the intense focus it took to write a book. He applauded and recognized my adoption of the family trade. Thanks Pops. (Dad's book, if you're interested, is "The Slope of Kongwa Hill.")

The women of my early life—Mom, Imelda Edwards, and sister Tamrah Lindsay Nicole Edwards. (*Full name published to rekindle sibling rivalry via embarrassment*)

I failed you countless times, yet you loved and love me. We have survived, and we are still here. Thank you for being you.

The village of adults who helped raise me. Ed and Leona Bridges. Glen and Heather Birnie Tickner. Keith and Felicity Hudson. Jim and Patti Scarborough. Mary Zahorecz. The brothers and sisters I never had … Dan, John and Dennis Bridges. Spencer and Evan Tickner. Natalie, Shastine, Stephen and Gareth Hudson. Garrett Scarborough. Paul and Eric Zahorecz.

Some of my schoolteachers spotted my talent with words, language, grammar, syntax and creative writing. Abraham Share, Rose Parrish, Edna Rountree, Dorothy Schneider, Nancy Beagle … very few of these were my English teachers, though! I haven't forgotten you, especially the ones who cared. Someday I'd like a chance to apologize for driving all of you crazy.

I owe Andrew Magliolo thanks for rescuing me from becoming homeless and destitute at the age of 20. Overweight, rudderless, addicted, broke and wasting away at a young age, I fell into the opportunity to be around a successful, accomplished speaker, actor and teacher. If he reads this is irrelevant; there's no way this book would have happened if he wasn't part of the story. He too noticed my verbal aptitude. Thank you, sir.

My uncle, John Madden (not *the* John Madden), became a long-lasting source of encouragement and inspiration. Particularly as my life came under the authority and care of Jesus Christ. A kind and doting uncle, John played an irreplaceable role in ushering my life into the presence of God. He prophesied and proclaimed that I was a writer after my dad's own heart. Americans do not usually win the accolades of erudite English (or South African, in John's case) observers. I'm honored to be among the fortunate few.

When I wore a soldier's uniform, close spiritual and physical allies like Seth Whatley, David De Rego, Ric Brown and others kept me in the fight long after I should have expired. I regret that I spent much of that time in a hollow religious fog. There remains much undone on my part for their benefit. Other men in uniform, like Roy Clayton and Bryan Legere, saw my talent and believed in me even while giving me a good-natured hard time about it. These guys wouldn't ever let me quit!

Professors at Pacific Lutheran University who refined my excessive verbiage deserve a nod – Amy Young, Diane Harney, Robert Wells, Art Land and Cliff Rowe. Thank you for being vicious with my superfluous language. Too many words make me a dull communicator. I also regret being such a pompous blowhard during my campus days. It's okay to be kind while being fully persuaded of things.

Cliff Rowe connected me with Tom Tangney, Josh Kerns, Ursula Reutin, Larry Rice, Tony Miner, David Boze, Michael Medved and everyone at KIRO/KTTH in Seattle, and John Carlson, Dojo and Wayne's World at KVI. I learned a boatload from all of you, and that was one of the first times networking so powerfully worked for me. I didn't have eyes to see it at the time, but the blindness has receded.

Over six years in the insurance business, I learned countless lessons in sales, persuasion, networking and so forth from my employers and colleagues: Jeff Kearin, Jonathan Cisneros, Angela Austin, Sandy Adams, Abrann Harris, Michelle Paul, Vicki Haworth, Karolyn James, Walker Clark, Emily Flemm, Christine Graf, Lacy Andrews, Trevor Campbell, Scottie Moffett, Merri-Sue Norris and Stephanie Corcoran. None of what I've accomplished happens without great people working behind the scenes and sharing what they know.

I am indebted to some of my strongest local, national and international marketing allies and friends. These people, each in small but noticeable ways, paved the broken road for this book to reach editing and printing. Thank you to my friend Alan Shimamoto for planting the seed long ago, suggesting I begin presenting and speaking on the subject, and for continued interest and insight as we moved the ball down the field (#GoBroncos).

Thank you to Sara Younger, who became a "protégé" of sorts and showed me just how much motivated people can "pass you up" when you teach them what they want to know. I am very proud of you and miss bringing the magic of personal relationships to people as we once did.

My network, my friends, my associates and clients: Sarah Hendry, Melanie Bakala, Andrew Barkis, Rick and Marie Nelsen, Garrett Gunderson, Michael Steadman, Mark Morgan, Terry Toth, Wes Martin, Christine Forrey, Tina Torfin, Tiana Kleinhoff, Samantha Styger, Ken McClarty, Michael Jameson, Valerie Waterland, Daryl Murrow, Sans Gilmore, Martha Wagner, Pam Pellegrino, Randy Luke, Martin McElliott, Josh and Jenny Mercer, Kevin Hayward, Brad Altman, Carlos Camargo, Matt Shields, Brandon Carter … I know I've forgotten some important names, but I'll exceed the word count if I don't slow down.

I owe my brothers from Wild At Heart Boot Camp a massive thanks for helping me shred my fear, doubt and discouragement many times–Dave Culbreath, Jeremy Tomlin, Michael Mercado and Jerry Raber. You are truly like-hearted kings with ready weapons and fierce mastery over darkness.

The priesthood at Ransomed Heart Ministries in Colorado Springs may never read this, but this book also wouldn't exist without the massive intervention of John and Stasi Eldredge, Morgan Snyder, Bart Hansen, Craig McConnell, Allen Arnold, Alex Burton, Karen Christakis and Sam, Blaine and Luke Eldredge.

The flood of personal development mentors in my life from 2017 is its own list of people to thank, but if there's one expert who instigated the whole thing, it's undoubtedly been Vince Del Monte. From coaching me out of 55 extra pounds and 15 percent extra body fat to helping me craft the very beginnings of my online business, I am proud to have you as a mentor and friend, as well as an ally in the Kingdom.

Riding in on this wave have come several wise and knowledgeable major influencer sources including Dan Lok, Bedros Keuilian, Craig Ballantyne, Rob Kosberg, Brittany Michalchuk and Jayson Gaignard. I have learned so much from all of you; I appreciate everything your lives and work have meant to me.

With those names came some of my favorite people– rising stars in their industries: Luis Diaz, John Carser, Luis Uribe, Cameron Hall, Mohammed Nahoori, Rob Westra, Carolina Marrelli, Marion Cain, Antonella Kahler, Katie Osterhoff, David Martinez, Sam Baker, Paul Rudzik and Femi Doyle-Marshall. If peer-to-peer accountability is the best kind of accountability, imagine what peer-to-peer inspiration does? I'm excited to see where we all end up. I look forward to our own days of influence.

The cavalcade continued as I logged my 10,000 hours of podcast guests. John Corcoran, Kevin Aillaud, Ron Carucci, Corey Blake, Giuseppe Grammatico, Matt Johnson, Ben Case, Ryan Miller, Marie Incontrera, Kevin Thompson, Kathleen Gage, Shawn Harper, Jill Valdez, Rabbi Daniel Lapin, Adam Connors, Tommy Miller … there are many more to name.

There is no leaving out the powerful "board of directors" I've acquired in joining the Iron Sharpens Iron Mastermind. Aaron Walker, Kevin Wallenbeck, Steve Kinsley, Scott Hooper, Chad Stokes, Chuck Wood, Raul Figueroa, Andy Misiura, Derek Champagne and Jeff Ristine have challenged and ushered me into a year of breakthrough.

Thank you to my most excellent clientele for trusting me with your voices and words: Aaron Walker and the View From the Top Team; Brian McRae and Mastermind St. Louis; Bill Sturm and Rausch Sturm; Bill Caskey and his team at Caskey Training; Dr. Andy Garrett and his team at AG-Thrive; David Hancock at Morgan James Publishing; and Luis Diaz of Podcast Domination.

My spiritual sons and younger brothers in the Young Adults discipleship group … Devon LeMaster, Jeshurun Roach, Quentin McDaris, Liam McDaris, Ryan Bradley, Scott McIntyre, Caleb Wilson, Jordan Ventura, Jordan McNair, Victor Hanna, Rod Dresser and Michael McAllister. You men bring bucketloads of joy into my life with your questions, energy and openness to life. Don't be like I was when I was younger, but you're welcome to join me where I'm headed.

Closer to home, I am indebted for a lengthy overwatch from my pastors, Jon and Fawn Cobler at the Church of Living Water in Olympia, Wash. It hasn't always been an easy job shepherding me, but you have done it with honor and grace I hope to return one day. Ditto Tim and Dhana Wimberly, Burt and Jan Smith, Steven and Jessica Mulkey, Ryan and Holly Schlecht, Steve and Joan Purdue, Chase and Holly Merrell and the rest of the pastoral staff.

The love and support of our family from my in-laws, Bill and Beth Dignon, deserves hearty applause. Time and again, you've provided a lot of support, encouragement and relief to us all. Everyone else wishes they had in-laws like you.

In the first edition of this book, I didn't sufficiently express my gratitude to my wife and children – Shannon, Grant and Chase. This book got completed in the margins of life and I appreciate their support and understanding as I worked to make it a reality.

My boys delight me daily with their energy, and especially in their maturing and learning to handle life on their own. I am proud of both of you. I hope this book becomes useful to you one day, even though it's the "old bull" writing.

Even more profoundly, I see how incredibly fortunate I am to have such a supportive, loving and loyal wife in Shannon. You can imagine that writing a book, launching an online business and creating a network ain't what it used to be … my bride handles this with such panache and grace despite my failures and setbacks. The written word will never do justice to a supportive and faithful wife.

And God Almighty, Jesus Christ, the King of Kings– where do I even begin to acknowledge all the fruit of the Kingdom you've grown in me? How can I tell of your presence, your goodness and your faithfulness in my life? How would I persuade someone of your mighty hand moving and even writing important portions of this book?

We've come a long way, you and I. It'd be nice to "look back and see how well I handled it all," but we both know it's only because of You that I'm standing here, accomplishing this, even after all my best attempts to plunge myself back into the mud.

Glory, then, is the only response fitting for you. Glory to your name. And may this book bring honor to you and your Kingdom.

Paul

CHAPTER 1

My Beginnings: From Awkward, Pushy Salesman to Radically Generous Entrepreneur

To begin this book chronologically would be a mistake. I can't tell you how I got started without first discussing where I was meant to end up. I didn't know where this was going when this began, and today I only know some extent of the outcome.

Becoming a Radically Generous Entrepreneur is a journey of faith. You hear its sound, you feel it, but you don't always know where it comes from. And you only find out where it's going gradually, in stages. That was the grand scheme of this journey: to discover and become my aspirational identity.

When I wrote "Business Beyond Business," I decided to make a client avatar out of the Radically Generous Entrepreneur. In hindsight, it was a mistake. That is more like the symbol of <u>where we can go together</u>, whether or not we actually exchange money. The avatar I sought needed to be someone much more concrete in the present moment.

The pathway lies in pursuing deep relationship with a rare kind of person. Usually, I do this by experiencing hundreds of relationships of varying substance. Some never get beyond casual greetings. Others progress out of the shallow end of the pool. But they only go far, often for reasons that make total sense.

Some friendships get into detail and depth. Peripheral to me are a select group of men, mainly fellow Christian entrepreneurs. Most of them don't know each other. But they mutually know me. We are transparent, authentic and vulnerable with one another. We share our personal and professional lives. We fight spiritual battles together. We contribute to each other's businesses.

Then there are relationships that go as deep as the bottom of the ocean. These people see in me what I fail to see in myself. They plow right through my humility. They insist on seeing the measure of glory God gives, as uniquely expressed through me. These people are very, very rare. I have perhaps a dozen of them in my life. Most people have none.

Okay, Fine. But What Do You DO?

I do two things well - . You could call me by my occupation—executive ghostwriter. I write content in your voice, which you can plug and play to build connection with your audience. But that isn't what this book is about. Plenty of other people also do ghostwriting. It's hardly a new thing.

There are people I know with whom I have relational capital and can call in some degree of favors. I can definitely pour value into them all day long. Sometimes they will reciprocate. Other times, I'll get my comeuppance from a third-party source that has nothing to do with it. But that's not unique either. Plenty of people experience things like that.

The gold in this book is this: there are people who know me. These are the hardest people to find. It's not clear scientifically how you locate them. The chemistry created by two living, breathing stories interacting at profound levels isn't easy to engineer. You may have experienced it. If you've ever been around someone whose interest in you made *them* more interesting than your own story, you know what I mean.

These people usually fire all key cylinders of the Radically Generous Entrepreneur at 80 percent or better. It took me a long time to find the one that went a thousand levels deep.

But I was meant to end up pursuing an aspirational identity in fellowship with others on a similar path, which brings us to the chronological starting place.

The "Pushy Salesman"

In the summer of 2013, I completed onboarding with Liberty Mutual Insurance in Tumwater, Wash. My branch manager, Abrann Harris, sat me down in his office to review my marketing plan. During that meeting, Abrann said something I've never forgotten. "We don't want you sitting around this office," he said. "The majority of your time should be spent out in the field. Networking, doing community events, being visible. If you're here, it should be to bind coverage on a policy, or meet with a client."

It sounded vague. But I'd been in unclear situations as an Army leader before. I knew it meant *something*, and it was incumbent on me to figure it out. So I researched local opportunities to network and meet people. I found several of them, and started my journey. The earliest memories I have were in Tumwater Rotary, the Thurston County Multiple Listings Sales Association and the Thurston County Chamber of Commerce's monthly forums.

It didn't take long to notice that people I met at these events felt uncomfortable around me. For one thing, I was a big, husky guy with a deep speaking voice and an intense stare. The soldier was still very strong in me. I wasn't good at putting people at ease, and I had just left behind a negative, micromanaged work environment in my previous job. There were spiritual knots that would take years to untangle.

What's worse, I thought my mission was to "sell, sell, sell." That's true, if you look at sales one-dimensionally. There's no "business" if you don't sell. "Feast or famine" had been the mantra of my previous employer. I knew Liberty would still review my performance at some point. I'd have to sell, to prove to them it was worth keeping me. My business card read "Sales Representative." At that level, it seemed obvious to me what needed to happen.

But the big mystery was that nobody at any of these events <u>wanted to buy</u>. Not even when I cornered them and they felt pressured to be polite. People began to avoid me. They knew what I wanted to talk about. They knew I was willing to get uncomfortable. They wanted no part of it. I wasn't afraid of rejection, but I could sense their awkwardness. So I backed off and spent a few months observing.

There weren't words in my vocabulary at the time to explain it. But I could sense that <u>whatever else people wanted</u>, they did NOT want to be sold.

Digital Advantage

My Liberty career never took off like I hoped it would. But there was a brief "spike" in the summer of 2014. I joined the Agency Alliance Mastermind, with Sean Matheis and Jonathan Garrick. This was the first time, but not the last, that masterminds would change my life.

Both men strongly influenced how I looked at business. Sean taught me how to craft simple, repeatable Facebook ad strategies. Those generated leads for the next three years of my career. Good leads, where I was not competing against other agents.

Meanwhile, Jonathan taught me the game of influence. He taught me how to carry myself in person and on social media. More than anything else at the time, Jonathan's others-centered approach resonated deeply. It took all the pressure out of selling insurance. As he taught me, "If you're going to put a video on Facebook, DO NOT talk about insurance. Nobody cares or wants to talk about it."

I enquired as to what to replace it with. He replied, "People want a chance to get to know you. Talk about your family. Hobbies, interests, places you go, people you meet. They already know what you do for a living. They can see it if you have it listed on your profile. What they *don't* know is what kind of man you are. Give them a chance to kick the tires."

Almost as quickly as I implemented his advice, my connection with the Olympia business community transformed. People no longer avoided me at networking events. Their interest and awareness of what I was up to increased. There was a great deal more enthusiasm at my presence, and several people seemed to gravitate toward me as a leader.

Everywhere I went, strangers would approach me to say, "I love your videos." I gained new clients who sent me instant messages to say, "I feel as though I already know you, even though we've never met in person." My lead generation on social media brought national attention to the office. I was ranked third overall in lead generation, and got invited to lead a training call for rookie

representatives. In 2016, my habit of blogging on LinkedIn led me to my first published work—an article in
Insurance Business America.

Boards of Education

I served on several boards during those years. The best
thing about nonprofit boards is they're usually stacked
with entrepreneurs. Employees mostly lack the freedom
to leave their workplaces to attend. But Abrann had given
the order—I was to be a ghost in my office. So I went out
and found opportunities to serve.

When I started volunteering with boards, it was awkward. Another task I simply tackled head-on and learned
as I went. No two boards or organizations are exactly
alike, no matter what their bylaws say. You can't turn a
board into a leads group, so don't go there with your "me
first" hat on.

I learned to use my knowledge and connections to be
resourceful to committee members. From there, people
often assume you're an expert in your field. It short-
ens the steps they take when they need help. They ask:
"Where will we get the right insurance coverage for this
event?" There are fewer obstacles when a very natural fit
with the right answer is in the same room. All the boards
I joined helped me make strides, land great clients and
open new relationships.

I also discovered that the bigger the charity, the more
involvement you get from senior community leaders. On
his podcast, author Jayson Gaignard said that "the way

to a rich man's heart is through his charity." I discovered this was true for some of Olympia's prominent, well-to-do families. I scratched their backs to help them raise funds. They would turn around and do business with me. Or they'd elevate me into rooms I had no business being in, apart from their invitation.

Preaching and Teaching

I hold no paid ministry role or qualifications. I've never been invited to speak in the church I attend. (Probably for good reason.) But I believe I have a spiritual gift of teaching from God. Why else would I have this James Earl Jones voice and love being onstage talking to an audience?

Teaching is the heart of the Bible. The word "Torah," which traditionally encompasses the first five books of Moses, literally means "teaching" in Hebrew. It's a great and noble calling, but it also requires humility if you're going to honor God.

Teaching forces you to be attentive to detail. Business audiences are typically full of "Type A" adults. Hard chargers, high performers and lovers of actionable steps based on sound principles. Teaching adults forced me to *think* about what I was going to say. How I was going to say it. Whether they were likely to care. How my content squared with reality.

In 2015 I began giving a free seminar, "Networking Intentionally." I taught it at local leads groups. It helped entrepreneurs become better at building relationships. If you watch the video I still keep on YouTube, you can hear some fundamentals of this book in what I shared. They comprised my earliest attempts at naming the values of my aspirational identity.

In this book, we'll unpack the Five Qualities of the Radically Generous Entrepreneur:

The Monastic Heart

I am fairly extroverted. I'm not afraid to talk to strangers. It doesn't take long for me to get a few layers deep with people. If it's the right person, I can make a lifelong friend of a stranger on a bus.

My maxed out networking habits produced a healthful "paring back" of that outgoing nature. Crowds no longer have the pull they used to because they're just crowds. "Small talk" at networking groups got stale. I got clearer on my personality. I realized a lot of my "performance" aspirations came from wanting applause. My extroverted side is much better expressed in small groups, especially entrepreneurial ones.

It was tempting to think of my gradual introversion as a liability, at least where networking is concerned. It's assumed extroverts get the lion's share of attention. After all, how can quiet people compete against someone loud and engaging?

I love it when people ask that. I've been teaching introverted entrepreneurs how to network for years. I'm so persuaded, in fact, that I believe the opposite is true: quiet professionals have every advantage in modern networking. Why wouldn't they? Our senses are bombarded around the clock by content, marketing and noise. We're starved for someone to listen to everything we bottle up inside. Who is likelier to get your attention these days—a nonstop talker, or someone who treats interacting with you like an exclusive interview?

Morgan Snyder of Ransomed Heart Ministries appeared on my podcast in late 2018. He's a powerful mentor in my life. I interviewed him about three primary relational styles. One of them, "Move Away," describes the introvert. I love how he defined it:

"These people have a reflective heart and soul. They're contemplative."

These ways brought enormous redemption to my tired, parched soul. I discovered they were enormously effective in business. I love how they've fundamentally changed my posture. Where I was desperate and needy, I can now relax and offer my best self. I'm not in a rush to sell. I don't feel threatened or disqualified by people ignoring me. And when I adopt the posture of a curious student, I don't usually elicit disregard.

Pro Bono Publicity

There's never been a worse time to "toot your own horn" in business than today. We have two succeeding generations flooding the workforce—Millennials and Generation Z. They both see right through it, and have all kinds of convenient ways of dodging the braggadocio.

There's never been a better time to have someone else praise you, either. Those same generations devour social proof and testimonials online in a way that doesn't occur to me. My Millennial friends tell me, "If I can't read reviews or watch testimonials, I won't buy." It's baffling. But it's true about them.

Early in my first mastermind experience, Jonathan Garrick reminded me of an eternal principle. I first read it in "How to Win Friends and Influence People," the Dale Carnegie classic. It states, "We are interested in others when they're interested in us." Jonathan reminded me of this by advising me how to use Facebook. He said, "If you're going to talk about business, talk about *somebody else's business*. Not your own."

Insurance sales made an ideal "training environment" for this. Nobody I knew wanted to discuss insurance anyway! So I started going to real estate open houses instead. I'd whip out my phone and do a video tour to promote the listing. I'd interview realtors and specialty contractors. Then I'd post it as a "Business Profile of the Week." If you can picture an insurance agent disguised as a journalist, you're on the right track.

Over time, I acquired a reputation for promoting other businesses. This made my disguise something more than a journalist; I was now a publicist, and one who didn't charge a fee. I didn't realize how much people appreciated this until my insurance career ended in June of 2018. My phone was inundated with condolences, offers of employment, business opportunities and people volunteering to connect me. It was a little too late; I'd already "hired myself" the same day I got fired. (Yes, I got fired.

For not selling well. I did a video on Facebook about it two days afterward. We tell the unvarnished truth around here; you'll like it.)

I'd originally tried podcasting as a conservative commentator in 2010. It was a failure, mainly because the fuel was my pride and self-righteousness. But, reborn as an influencer, I figured a podcast would make a good compliment to my first book, "10 Secrets to Networking Success." So, in the late summer of 2018, after six years of silence, I got back behind the mic.

I had no idea podcasting would become the vehicle to "scale" my skill for building influence. I was just babbling into the mic. My show kicked off with a bunch of solo episodes. The only thing that changed was the content. Instead of politics, I was issuing monologues about a combination of business and spirituality.

Then, in September, my new business coach Vince Del Monte got on my case. "Why are you just there by yourself?" he demanded to know. "You should be interviewing people." So, I started approaching people from my old and new networks to appear on the show. Internet marketing guru Paul Getter was the first to appear, followed by business coaches Craig Ballantyne and Brittany Michalchuk.

I made conversations with fellow members of Vince's 7-Figure Mastermind, such as Luis Diaz, Brian Moncada and Cameron Hall. Here in Olympia, business coaches Alan Shimamoto and Daryl Murrow also made great guests. Soon, it began to snowball. In December I crossed over into the Best Seller Publishing Mastermind. I interviewed CEO Rob Kosberg, followed by several of his author-clients. I started connecting his publicity team with other podcasts where I got interviewed, making their jobs easier. In turn, they would reach out regularly with new prospective guests to interview.

Podcasting was the absolute best part of everything I tried. I never monetized my show. Not, at any rate, in the sense of selling products, generating leads or paid advertising. During this season, I still had no compelling offer. But I added listeners, downloads and notoriety every month over 14 months. The guests got more interesting, more prominent and more varied.

At some point, it became clear. My habit of interviewing and promoting others was doing the same thing I'd been doing at real estate open houses. I didn't need a massive audience or for 400 people to buy a coaching product. My guests are my audience. By schmoozing them for half an hour about their books, products and programs, I was building rapport and endorsement. I just needed to keep doing it until the right person took note of it.

In the spring of 2019 I got a note from Patrick Antonucci. We've been friends since he interviewed me for his podcast, *Dad Hackers*. He recommended I interview Aaron Walker, founder and president of a company called View From the Top. After doing a little research, I discovered Aaron was a close friend of Dave Ramsey, the legendary financial guru and radio host.

Aaron made an even better guest than an impression. He came aboard to discuss his mastermind group, Iron Sharpens Iron. We had a wonderful exchange. On the post-interview chat, he mentioned that he planned to release a new product in the fall called "The Mastermind Playbook." I promised to follow up in September to book him for another interview.

I didn't know it, but that interview was the end of the beginning.

Podcasting continued well. In August 2019 I welcomed Rabbi Daniel Lapin to the show. By this time I was able to simulcast interviews over Facebook Live. Several people in my audience were astonished to see me casually chatting with a man who normally appears in front of nationally televised commentators like Glenn Beck and Sean Hannity.

Conscious Capitalism founder Corey Blake rejoined me for a second interview in September. He'd just completed the documentary "It's About Time." It chronicled the work of PayActiv, a now-famous tech firm that solved the paycheck-to-paycheck crisis of America's underclass. I got the recommendation from Corey to interview Safwan Shah, the CEO of PayActiv. It led to the rebranding of the show's second season. I would now focus a chunk of my energy on executives and entrepreneurs in the technology sector.

In February 2020, John Eldredge, my longtime mentor from Ransomed Heart, appeared for an interview. We discussed his newest book, "Get Your Life

Back." His appearance was the product of what I call "crockpot bookings." These take <u>longer</u> to get guests that are much more difficult to land. But they point back to my same old strategy of worming my way into people's consciousness.

Not-For-Profit IS For-Profit

Civic and charitable causes are, without question, staples of the Radically Generous Entrepreneur. It would be quite out of character to avoid them.

Back in my insurance days, I got involved in two key nonprofit groups. The Association of the United States Army (AUSA) was an obvious fit. I'm a veteran, and I'd always wanted to do for soldiers what was done for me when I wore the uniform. So I spent many occasions raising funds, serving soldiers and families, and attending military-related events where local civilian leaders were invited. This got me into closer and friendlier interactions with generals and senior leadership at Joint Base Lewis-McChord (JBLM) than I'd ever been while wearing the uniform.

The cities that surround JBLM are known for their patriotism and support of the military. Participating in AUSA gave me an inexhaustible list of opportunities to meet and connect with people. It took me all over the Puget Sound Region, from attending a lecture by the commanding general of JBLM at the University of Washington to a private meeting with Cheryl Selby, Mayor of Olympia, in 2016.

The Miss America Scholarship Pageant was more of a surprise. I'd never had anything to do with pageants. My sister, Tamrah, did not compete in them growing up. I knew of no history of it in my family. But I got into it by doing the kind of thing you'll learn about in Chapter Five. I networked with people who "appeared" to be average citizens of Lewis County, south of where I live. They turned out to be active board members of the pageant. They needed a male emcee.

Emceeing pageants reminded me of the power of on-stage performance. Parents and community leaders of Lewis and Thurston counties were far more receptive to meeting me. Participating in "dramatized reality" affords an entrepreneur something competitors can't match. I wouldn't equate it with "star power," but I would say there's a parallel. Large crowds of people paying attention to you does something to human perception. It has a psychological effect on how we "rank" people.

I entered both groups to serve and meet new people, but left with far more than I'd bargained for. I ended up getting publicity, community partnerships and high-level connections, as well as plenty of clients, including the biggest client of my insurance career.

Dream Networker

Best Seller Publishing got me two television appearances for my book. In both cases, the hosts paid attention to my "Five Tips for Networking with Dream

Connections." There's something about it that's easily digestible for TV audiences.

The key to understanding networking today is found in the fifth tip, "Focus on the Farm Team." It's a handy way to remember that if you perform the other four tips with the <u>average</u> person you meet, you'll know what to do when you get a "whale." So, what you'll learn in that chapter can be implemented immediately. Don't wait until you're standing in front of a celebrity or national leader. Radically Generous Entrepreneurs do this for anyone.

To close the earlier loop, this is how I became the emcee of the Miss Lewis and Miss Thurston County Pageants. I was doing a trade show in Lewis County, and volunteered to take over the role of announcing raffle prizes. It seemed like a small gesture. But to Melinda Wilkes, the event organizer, it was huge. She hated public speaking; I loved it. The rest is history. Melinda will not make national headlines, but I helped and served her anyway.

Alan Shimamoto used this same approach with me. We first met at a Chamber of Commerce leads group. He learned I was a fan of the Denver Broncos. They'd just gone home with tails between their legs in Super Bowl 48 at the hands of the Seattle Seahawks. But Alan cheerfully offered me a free ticket to watch the teams' upcoming rematch at CenturyLink Field.

We referenced that exchange when I interviewed Alan on the podcast. He said, "If I would have led with selling product, we could have had a 'one-and-done' conversation. Chances are, we wouldn't have had the strong relationship we have. Instead, we developed a friendship first. Later, you ended up doing business with me."

I still use some of the products Alan sold at the time—AdvoCare—to this day, six years after he invited me to tag along to a football game. He could have sold those tickets and made money. I wasn't going to bring him national attention; it didn't matter. He focused on the farm team.

The other four "tips" for networking with dream connections are part of what you'll learn, or intuitively figure out, from this book. You need to approach networking the way a master fisherman "angles" to catch a fish; you can't do relational business through transactional experiences. So I tell people, "Be an angler."

To reduce your self-interest to an appropriate level, I also counsel people to "keep your ear to the ground." This is like being a "scout" for your network—paying attention to opportunities and people you meet on others' behalf. What gave me such easy access to people's favor was an expectation I created that I'd show up with a gift of some kind. Encountering me usually meant there was an introduction, a connection, an invitation to an exclusive event or a pearl of wisdom in tow.

Another way to do this is what I call "done-for-you publicity." This is more specialized, and usually applies when you are a customer of people in your network. You purchase their stuff, review their products online, attend their events, grant them interviews or publicity and otherwise promote the hell out of them. Put simply, become an evangelist for products and services you dig. Don't simply enjoy them for yourself; share them with the world.

If all those things fail, I remind people that you can always ask the "Three Big Questions." Behave like a curious interviewer, like Oprah Winfrey or Howard Stern. Dig deep into people's lives by asking, "What's going well for you lately?" Celebrate their wins with them, and keep digging to find what most inspires or motivates them. Dig deeper by asking, "What's not going so well for you?" Unearth their struggles, frustrations and pain points <u>so you can match them with your network!</u> It's amazing how much you can become a "broker" for people if you'll just be curious and stop talking about yourself.

And don't forget to put icing on the cake by asking, "What are you looking forward to?" Reorient them to the future and the good things they can see coming over the horizon.

Persuasive in Print

Radically Generous Entrepreneurs are unbeatable in print. I've never met one who does a lousy job of communicating. Usually, they understand how easy it is to mishandle the written word. They're obsessed with making sure it doesn't happen on their watch.

Let's face it, we live in a glut of written information and content. Our e-mail inboxes are flooded every day.

If it doesn't happen there, we get it through direct messages, texts, snapchats, what have you. But Radically Generous Entrepreneurs have a knack for getting heard more often than others competing for attention.

Embodying this skill was Major General Craig Whelden, a retired Army officer I met through Best Seller Publishing. His book, "Leadership: The Art of Inspiring People to Be Their Best," contained several passages about how he'd learned to do it. I interviewed him for my show in the fall of 2019. His stories and observations prove the points and substance of this concept.

This ethic also calls for a strategic approach to creating content. It's no longer enough to write for its own sake; we must now command the attention of our readers by writing something valuable. With the celebrity industry as decimated as it is, fewer and fewer people can just hop on social media and unleash their stream of consciousness. Whatever you're going to say, you'd better be able to communicate it clearly and authentically.

Learning the art of copywriting taught me to enter the conversation the buyer is already having in their head. We must, at any given moment, be versatile enough to speak to conditions as they presently exist. Moreover, we need to be able to demonstrate an emotionally intelligent connection with the reader. We must be able to intuit their fears, anxieties, hopes and dreams through each stroke of our keyboard. And our written offering should speak directly to them, offering a clear alternative to the ambiguity the human soul abhors.

The Curator

Radically Generous Entrepreneurs are selective and pro-
tective of their relationships. They don't associate with
just anybody. They understand accepting one opportunity means rejecting another. Choosing one person to
connect with means excluding everyone else.

Even as they're selective of their circle, Radically
Generous Entrepreneurs NEVER give up on meeting
new people. Building new connections. Adding value to
others. Promoting, celebrating and supporting people.
Human relationships are spiritual things, which means
they can't be measured or quantified. You really have no
idea how much they can grow; all you can do is keep
nourishing them.

With nearly everyone who came on my podcast, I
tried the same thing. I made sure they got more value
after the interview. I'd connect them with three or more
people they didn't already know. If they had a show,
I'd find them new guests. If they were serial guests, I'd
find them new shows. If they were looking for certain
audiences, I'd steer them toward certain shows. If they
needed certain services, I'd recommend the best people I
knew. Over and over.

I began to notice certain people consistently followed up in response to my gestures. Some people took
them seriously. Others didn't. But by the time Aaron
Walker showed up for our second interview, he was part
of a much shorter list. I'd decided to "curate" my list of
people for whom I'd do full-throttle introductions.

Super-strong relationships are like my hobby, building muscle. Isolated focus on them causes growth. You need to sow heavily where you reap the greatest reward, but you cannot give up sowing. Without really knowing it at the time, I was building a groundswell of value. I would have continued doing it the same way if Aaron had disappeared back to his own life. But he didn't.

I'll tell you the rest of that story in Chapter Four.

But it might do good to mention, my connection with Aaron is a huge part of the reason you're reading this. He introduced me to David Hancock, my publisher at Morgan James. The scrawny, malnourished novice effort of "10 Secrets to Networking Success" reaches full maturity in this, its third edition—"Influencer Networking Secrets."

It's time to reveal the secrets. The secrets of how influencers network, and secrets of how to network with influencers.

CHAPTER 2 -
The Monastic Heart

Be a Magnet, Not a Pusher

My post-military career began in insurance sales. In some ways, it mirrored that of Ned Ryerson, the caricatured insurance salesman of the movie "Groundhog Day."

I went to see the movie in theaters with friends back in the early 1990s. Even before I knew anything about insurance, there was something about Ned that resonated with me. Actor Stephen Tobolowsky had an interesting comment about how he prepared for the role:

"I ask myself this about any part: 'What is my greatest hope? What is my greatest fear?' In this case, I thought, 'My greatest hope is that Phil Connors would

remember me, and be my friend.' And my greatest fear was being neglected, alone and put down."

Now, does that sound like a description of a pushy salesman? You hope to become memorable to people. Especially if they'll refer you to their friends. And your biggest fear is that everyone will avoid you, ignore you or turn on you. Those were certainly on my mind as I began to build my network.

(This goes way beyond the occupation of sales, by the way. This was a theme throughout my life. I was born to think deeply about this. Mainly so you could have some entertaining reading. But I digress.)

Pushers

Pushers are just what they sound like. Drug dealers and loan sharks are extreme examples. These people try to push things that can only be pulled, and vice versa. In my early days, I kept trying to steer the conversation toward insurance. You could have told me at the time, "People don't go to networking groups to buy insurance." But it wouldn't have mattered. I needed to hustle, make a buck and my vehicle was selling insurance.

It got marginally better at trade shows. There, I could at least be forgiven for having a sales agenda. I was standing behind a table with a corporate logo, prize giveaways and sign-up sheets. People would talk … but they wouldn't last long once I asked them about their insurance. And those were the ones that stopped to talk! Over time, I realized sales was no longer simply a "numbers game." The more I frequented trade shows, the less people would stop at my table. Even if I offered big prizes like Seattle Seahawks tickets. It was the mid 2010s, and the internet was reshaping how people thought about marketers.

There were occasions where all people had to hear was the word "insurance" and they'd immediately become defensive. One time, I set up a business meeting with the general manager of Olympia's largest health club. I was only there to secure a free membership for the winner of the Miss Thurston County Pageant; I had no intention of discussing insurance. But the manager asked what I did for a living. When I told her, she immediately told me who currently handled the club's insurance, adding how happy they were with the service. As in, "Don't even bring it up." Sheesh.

So, at a certain point, I dropped the subject completely. Insurance salesmen are, unfortunately, caricatured for a reason. They're selling a product most people don't understand, and wouldn't ordinarily buy. People resent being compelled to purchase it. The product itself is a highly imperfect bandage to the incurable wound of our negligence and ignorance. Most salespeople don't last very long because they don't understand that the insurance isn't actually the product being sold; <u>they are</u>.

Whatever the reasons were that people didn't want to talk about insurance, I got one thing right. I stopped talking about it. If your marketplace tells you repeatedly, "Don't push this on us!" … you had better listen.

Magnets

People are drawn toward Magnets because Magnets don't look at them like "transactions." Pushers do that, and it bugs me. Their main concern is swapping products for money. All they care about is the temporal and immediate. To pushers, other people only matter so far as they can do something for the pusher straightaway.

Magnets are different. Magnets see people more like untapped reservoirs of knowledge, ideas, passions and connections–particularly if they can sense "fellow" Magnets. When you're a Magnet, you use what is within your power to bring people closer to you.

Magnets take a long view of nearly everything, especially people: "Where might a friendship with that person lead?"

Radically Generous Entrepreneurs trend "magnetic." They pull people toward them with selflessness, clarity and knowledge. They don't push or manipulate people around them into buying a product. They don't waste time with idle chit-chat. When meeting people, a Radically Generous Entrepreneur asks intelligent questions. They don't ramble about the weather, grumble about politics or prattle about sports scores.

Magnetism: A Practical Example

An irony emerged over time from my "code of silence" on the topic of insurance. The less I talked about it, the more people wanted to talk about it anyway.

As I said, Magnets create a gravitational pull. It's a

form of reverse psychology. Have you heard of the term "cognitive dissonance"? It's defined as "having inconsistent thoughts, beliefs or attitudes, especially relating to behavioral decisions or attitude change." People subconsciously had to wonder: "This man is an insurance salesman. Why doesn't he try to sell me insurance? Has he forgotten how he's supposed to behave?" So, in an amusing reversal of fortune, they began to pester me about it.

Believe it or not, there came a day when I knew I'd reversed the poles on this. One of my biggest clients, Lacey City Councilman Mike Steadman, invited me to watch his son compete in mixed martial arts at a local dojo. I took my eldest son, I left my business cards at home. There was absolutely no sales or marketing agenda on my mind going into the occasion, unless you want to count maintaining good relations with one of my best clients.

I knew some of the other people there. You always do when you go out in Olympia. Mark Morgan was there. We were friends through our shared hobby of bodybuilding, but he'd also referred me a huge client. So you could say I now had a very informal agenda of chumming with clients and referral partners.

We sat around cracking jokes prior to the match. As time passed, several people in Mike's vast association of friends came and sat with us. One by one, Mike introduced me: "This is Paul, he's my insurance agent." True to philosophy by this time, I simply remained pleasant, shook hands and made casual conversation. I didn't breathe a word about insurance … but Mike's friends certainly did! Some of them began a comical barrage. It alternated between serious questions about insurance and tongue-in-cheek "insurance salesman jokes." (Yes, they do have them.)

The climax came when one of them asked me a serious question and I didn't know the answer. They began to giggle as I thought about it, and chide me for not being up to speed on my work. Playing along with feigned offense, I turned around like an indignant prospect being harassed by a pushy insurance salesman. I said through a grin, "I didn't come here to talk about insurance, I want to enjoy the boxing match!" Everyone laughed, and I realized I'd become completely detached from the sales agenda.

De-Magnetization

Not many people describe themselves as shallow. But we can become that way when anxiety overrides common sense. That's part of what happened to me in my early years; I was in such a rush to "get something going" that I treated people like transactions. Not surprisingly, I lost a lot of deals and served many customers poorly in my desperation to acquire new accounts.

Looking back at it now, I come to a familiar refrain. Business is a spiritual activity. We're not trained in the Western world to think of it this way. Any interaction between two human beings has a spiritual component. It can be a dead one, if you like. But it's not mere clashing of sound waves generated by molecules proceeding from mouths of flesh. It's the interaction of *souls* that produces energy—confidence, feelings of well-being and willingness to part with resources.

I didn't understand this well enough to treat my role as a spiritual practice. Therefore, I always assumed that I had to "strike fast" to keep customers before their interest trailed off. I never knew why many of them approached me in the first place. I didn't bother to inquire, and paid minimal attention when they told me. That was a tremendous mistake. If I'd understood how valuable it was, I wouldn't have skipped over so many details and subtleties that could have made it a far more successful venture.

I was nearing the end of my insurance career when I realized I'd become hollow inside. Though I'd learned so much from my time in sales, it simply remained a false identity I'd turned to during dark economic times. Personal entropy had plagued me throughout the journey, and one clear indicator of personal entropy is shallowness in relationships. As this light went on in my soul, I resolved to stop doing business at the surface level. From now on, I'd swim in the deep end.

Radically Generous Entrepreneurs swim in the depths of interaction. They have three observable, magnetic values that make people go, "Hmmm …" These essences quietly distance the person from everyone else around them:

Depth
Confidence
Preparation

Depth refers mainly to an appetite for understanding motives. As an example, I'd occasionally meet someone who disliked networking. They'd react to my enthusiasm for it by saying something like, "I don't have time for networking."

The odd thing was they usually said this against the backdrop of networking! Remember, more than 80 percent of my time as an insurance agent was spent out of the office. Nobody came to visit me, except to transact business or make policy changes. If I wanted new business, I'd have to find people on neutral ground. In my mind, "networking" included visiting professionals wherever they'd meet me. In their offices and establishments. Business lunches. Fundraisers. Board meetings. Social gatherings. These were the places people told me, "I don't have time for networking."

I don't believe they had no time for networking. They just didn't like networking groups, which is far more understandable. They knew the power of relationships. They wanted more "power partners" in their lives. They were just far more attuned than I was to the unlikelihood of finding them at networking groups. One reason I dive heavily into the personal emptiness of my journey is that I believe most people are battling a similar problem somewhere. If they themselves aren't dealing with it, they're probably working for / with / over someone who is, and they're eager to understand the origin of the problem.

The Radically Generous Entrepreneur discovers newer, smarter ways of building relationships. They tap into those emotional reasons concealed by surface answers like "I don't have time for networking." They solve the problem, often through trial and error. Once they have the new path, they take others along for the ride. If you want to know how to network with depth and attention to detail, my friend Adam Connors teaches courses on it.

Confidence is a Radically Generous Entrepreneur's best friend. But you'd be surprised at how people think confidence is developed.

Some people think I'm a born public speaker and orator. It's true that I come from an erudite ancestry of English, leadership personalities. I was never shy as a child, and that did not change with adulthood. The military required me to speak publicly. I've had a long succession of great mentors who have helped me improve what I say and how I say it.

But my confidence would disappear entirely if I was asked to give a speech on nuclear physics or software engineering. I'm completely vacant on either topic. If I'm good at projecting confidence, it's because I stay in my lane. As Clint Eastwood famously said, "A man's got to know his limitations." A good rule of thumb I've learned for confidence is <u>never speak outside your own experience</u>.

Does this mean, then, that you can't project confidence unless you're the expert? By no means! The opposite is truer still. Curiosity is the soft end of the stick with confidence. It is not foolish to be totally ignorant of a subject, and yet exude curiosity about it. People who do this brim with confidence. They are *learning*. Expanding their knowledge base. They're not ashamed to say, "Help!" or "I don't know!" They understand the world is set up in such a way to create *interdependence* between human beings. Radically Generous Entrepreneurs specialize in a skill, and celebrate others who possess skills they lack.

Confidence is itself a skill set. A muscle that can be trained, grown and molded. Particularly through coaching.

My friend Kevin Aillaud goes by the moniker "The Alpha Male Coach." Smoothly spoken and casually vulnerable, Kevin's command of mindset is exceptional. He teaches men to cultivate their "inner alpha," characterized mainly by confidence.

"Freed from psychological fear, you see order and chaos both as normal," he told me in an interview. "The natural mind freaks out in the presence of chaos, and takes order for granted. But for the alpha, value comes from existence itself, rather than selfish, political, mob or group interests. When we overcome the illusion of scarcity, we realize that fear is just an emotion in our minds."

In other words, if you don't walk around with fear in the first place, you have nowhere to go but up. Kevin continued, "Liberation from fear of people judging you is never weakness, and always strength. When you let fear of people's opinions go, you're free from it and flooded with confidence. You're honest, you *want* people to judge you, because you know that their judgments reflect nothing whatsoever on you."

I spent most of the last 18 years in bad shape, driven by voices that squarely blamed me for one thing or another. If I heard my former military supervisors, I was at fault for not knowing things no one taught me. If it came from my former insurance employer, I felt "useless" without high sales volume. My internal lower self, the flesh, repeated and dwelt on it daily. Psychologically, this is called "endless self-rumination," an extremely destructive habit common to people who place a high premium on deep, personal and intimate relationships.

In recovering from these tendencies, I gave a derisive nickname to the voice that robbed me during my insurance years: The Spirit of False Urgency. Confidence in business (or anything else) simply has no room for being in a constant rush, and I was always in one. Gunning the engine to squeeze the last few sales at the end of the month. Carried along by anxiety, accusation, shame, fear and scarcity. The cruel irony was inevitable: I got half the results for twice the work. And every job I held ended with mixed results — some truly positive growth, and a lot of unresolved issues.

Radically Generous Entrepreneurs execute on a diligent, thorough schedule. They're thoughtful before, during and after the working day. They aren't rushing to try and capture as much of the market as they can. They see work as an important component of life, but not the "be all and end all." They reject the rampant workaholism of the Western entrepreneur class. They break with our deep-seated cultural "agreements" that success is entirely up to us, and that we're therefore weak or defective if it doesn't happen right away.

As for preparation, I've used the example set by President Ronald Reagan for years. Reagan is famous for iconic quotes like "Tear down this wall!" and a nonchalant self-confidence on camera. His casual quips and avuncular use of stories endeared him to millions of Americans. He led and celebrated a time of enormous national renewal in America, but more importantly, he made it look so *easy*. Reagan was as memorable for his playfulness as for any moving speech he ever gave.

Not much is said — dare I say *noticed* — about Reagan's habits of <u>preparation,</u> which led to those memorable moments. I don't claim to be a presidential historian. But I've read a fair amount of biographies, articles and accounts of his life in entertainment and politics. He wasn't so relatable and affable by accident. He stood out from your average politician by leaps and bounds. There's no denying the authenticity he brought to the role. But he was also very prepared.

To understand President Reagan, consider his career experience as a radio sports announcer. He became a B-movie actor, a Hollywood anti-communist, a speaker/trainer for General Electric, and, of course, governor of California. Reagan had spent a lifetime in front of audiences of all kinds, doing work at which he excelled. This means he spent even more time *rehearsing*. He learned from audience responses that confidence is a byproduct of extensive, detailed preparation. It was his *craft* to appear smoothly before a camera.

Entering politics, Reagan saw that humor and wit made fantastic tools for retaliating against his opponents. He began scripting comedic observations into his speeches. By the time he was elected president in 1980, he was already well known for simplifying complicated arguments into one-liners. On "The Tonight Show" in 1978, he quipped: "How come when we spend our money, it's inflationary, but when the government spends our money, it isn't?"

In campaigns and in office, Reagan was known to spend hours rehearsing jokes and speeches. He became "The Great Communicator" because he was *prepared*. He was forged in bringing characters to life on radio and camera. He was shaped and molded in ideological struggle, competing for the hearts and minds of American voters.

I ask you: If an extroverted, charismatic leader like Ronald Reagan needed hours of preparation to exude charm and wit, what makes you think you can just show up and do it? Why should you hide behind the label of introversion if the cost is tremendous opportunities that would help you grow your influence? I maintain that many times, this is what got me invited to the private rooms and unique gatherings. I simply took time to think about how to show up at networking events, or when I wanted something from someone.

Shyness, anxiety, or plain preference for solitude may give you a shortage of natural charisma. But *nothing* can stop you from <u>preparing</u> to move with confidence in the marketplace. As Seth Godin reminds us in his book "This Is Marketing," "We don't remember what we hear. We don't remember what we see. We don't even remember what we do; we remember what we *rehearse*."

Hear me now: This doesn't necessarily mean rehearsing lines and jokes! It can mean rehearsing a certain habit, like I did, of showing up with something useful or beneficial for others. That takes more than a few swings, especially if you're going to an event and you aren't sure who's going to be there. How do you prepare to benefit someone you've never met?

How I Prepare

I have to confess, I could prepare a lot more often. I don't do as much public speaking as I used to. But it takes practice to develop *any* interpersonal skill, not just public speaking.

Do you remember my three favorite questions? It took me several months of forgetting before they became a habit. Now I use them (or some version of them) reflexively. With some people, I get the perfect moment to use the original. "What's going well for you lately?" With others, it feels forced and awkward to say it that way. So I became creative with the wording. Recently I switched it to, "So, what's the best part about being you right now?" I got three paragraphs in response.

In some TV interviews I did for "Business Beyond Business," the hosts asked about the role of effective communication in business. I made a point of telling them, "Businessmen and women need to learn to think like journalists." By this, I mean you should practice the Five Big Questions of Journalism: Who, What, Where, When and Why/How. If you can keep those simple words in your head, sooner or later you'll start asking the right questions.

Once people reply to your question, you need to train yourself to listen for "bullet points." These can be things that excite the person you're speaking toor that intrigue you to ask more questions. Either way, digging deeper into what someone tells you builds layers of relationship. So let's say you ask someone, "What's going well for you lately?" and they answer, "I got five new clients this week."

Move into journalist mode here. "Really? Who were they? Anyone I know?" *Pause for their answers.* "How did you get them? Who was the source of the referral?" Now let's say they dodge and say, "Well, we got them from Facebook leads." *Now you have a new angle.* "Really? That's awesome. Tell me this, though. Some people I know say Facebook ads don't work for them. What are you doing differently that's turning over business?"

This isn't difficult. This is exactly what's taking place in my brain as I talk to someone.

Punxsutawney Phil

Ned Ryerson remained a pusher throughout "Groundhog Day." But the main character, Phil Connors, became a Magnet. Despairing of his long season reliving the same day over and again, Phil turned to improving himself. He learned to play the piano and ice sculpt (preparation). He became appreciative of beauty through poetry and music (depth). He was helpful to his fellow man. He gave the broadcast speech of his career, narrating the groundhog festivities (confidence).

In the final scenes, Phil's magnetism took over the entire town of Punxsutawney. He delivered a dazzling piano solo at the community hall. A parade of townspeople grateful for his good deeds interrupted his dance with Rita, his love interest. You could sense her attraction and interest in him skyrocketing as the layers compounded. When it came time for the bachelor auction, Rita spent every penny in her wallet to bid on him.

Phil got auctioned off to Rita, fell in *true* love with her … and they woke up to February 3rd. Self-effacing, self-sacrificing, generous and vivacious, Phil overcame his shallow, snobbish, self-centered beginnings. He discovered, as my old pastor Shane Rogers said, that "The meaning of life … is a life that has meaning."

That's what it means to be a Magnet instead of a Pusher.

You care about the depths. When people say or do certain things, you want to know why. The heart matters to you. The timing, placement, tonality and technique all factor into the delivery.

You radiate confidence. As Kevin Aillaud said, chaos and order are both normal to you. You can be an expert or a novice, and you don't feel exalted or condemned. You care more about wanting others to succeed and work you out of a job. What makes other people panic is a matter of routine for you. Difficult things are not "easier" for you. *But you are much easier to be around when things get difficult.* You embody the old Latin saying "Virtus Tentamine Gaudet." Translated, it means "Strength Rejoices in the Challenge."

For preparation, you make Boy Scouts look unready. You're as prepared to artfully confess ignorance as you are to humbly display prowess. Very few things catch you off guard. Others feel safe around you, even if they are unprepared. They learn that the only wrong answer with you is dishonesty. And the best complaint they can make is to propose a solution. Your responses, tonality and pace move steadily. You never walk into a room without something to give. Your answers are thoughtful, including ones that begin, "To be honest, I don't know that I can answer you right away …"

So, if you desire the path of the Radically Generous Entrepreneur, Rule #1 is Be a Magnet, Not a Pusher.

CHAPTER 3 -
Golden

Pro Bono Publicity

My father kept a copy of "How to Win Friends and Influence People" in his library. I remember reading it for the first time, fascinated with its insight into our condition. This quote from the author, Dale Carnegie, always stuck with me: "We are interested in others when they're interested in us." If I remember correctly, it can be found in a chapter where Carnegie recalled seizing occasions to compliment or inquire with curiosity about people he met. The thrust of the chapter was to become genuinely interested in the people around you.

Learning this lesson in face-to-face networking created a wellspring of opportunities. Understanding that technology enables us to do it globally is a game changer. You can "scale" networking by showing sincere interest in people without a production budget or a creative team. Then you can multiply value for anyone with an internet connection who wants to watch or listen.

Once I understood this principle, the dividends started racking up – and *kept* racking up. The old saying goes, "The more you do something, the more of it you'll get." I found opportunities increased with each practice round. You start out with simple ways of promoting your fellow entrepreneurs. Giving them shout-outs at networking groups. Sending them referrals. But soon, you're facilitating high-level introductions that lead to major contracts. Deals worth thousands or millions of dollars.

It's also my experience that if you do enough of this, you'll eventually reach a "new bottom rung." I did this for so long in Olympia that it reached a saturation point. I couldn't go any further if I remained an employee rather than an owner. But I also couldn't keep doing what I was doing and expecting a different result. I'd reached the lowest rung of the next ladder.

This became apparent when I went to New York City in November 2018 for Vince Del Monte's mastermind. I got shredded in the hot seat, and joined my friend Femi Doyle-Marshall for lunch afterward. I was dispirited. The coach panel had once again eaten me for breakfast (after a grilling in Toronto in August). I felt like I had nothing to offer. The only thing I had that showed signs of life was a fledgling podcast adding listeners, little by little.

Femi reminded me, "What you've done up until now worked in Olympia. But now you're in a room full of people playing at a much higher level."

I replied, "Yes, but to me that simply means everything I've learned can take me so far and no further."

Femi wasn't fooled. "No. What you learned there has an application here. It was all preparation for a new season of learning."

Femi was right. I went back into the conference center of the Stewart Hotel in Manhattan … and networked my butt off. I snapped photos with people. I did mini-interviews. I invited people to be on my show. I gave away every last copy of my book that I'd brought, personally autographed. I did everything I knew how to do … and the work could resume. It just took me a while to realize I was on the next bottom rung.

Pro Bono Publicity should characterize every stage of the Radically Generous Entrepreneur's journey, especially the beginning. When you have no marketing budget, you haven't defined your target client, your unique hook or even your offer. If you're absolutely empty-handed, you can still promote other entrepreneurs. You can still act as an unpaid publicist. The one thing you can't afford to forget is your "position" on the ladder of success.

Zero-Based Marketing Budget

Isn't it annoying, the price you pay to advertise? Especially on dinosaur formats like newsprint, TV and radio. Social media leveled that playing field to some degree. But even their advertising became stale and predictable after a while. The marketplace has adapted; everyone knows to look to see if a post is "sponsored" or "promoted."

My father was a career advertising executive. It does work; if it didn't, as many are fond of saying, businesses wouldn't keep doing it. This isn't a knock on the profession or the product. But I enjoy how my friend Brian McRae words it: "Paid advertising is the price you pay for being mediocre."

Let the reader understand! Brian's comment reflects on *sponsors*, not the advertising vehicle. He means that paid advertising is our attempt to bypass investment of time and effort into building quality relationships. I'm guilty as charged. In 2015 I made one of the dumbest decisions ever. I spent an obscene amount of money on radio ads for my insurance business. I ran two related campaign messages for six months. As my friend Michael McCormick said about his paid advertising: "Not. One. Lead." Imagine what I *could* have used that money to do for the people in my immediate network!

So come, let us reason together. Especially if you're new in business and don't have the budget. How can we "advertise" without paying confiscatory advertising rates?

The answer is, we turn ourselves into the advertising <u>vehicle</u>, and trust that it will open doors for us embodying the <u>commercial</u> along the way. We don't charge a penny to connect people with our audience. We get on a bullhorn that gets attention — we start a podcast, an e-mail list, a blog or perhaps an industry publication.

We shill for people, products and services we believe in and appreciate.

Or we start our own specialized form of networking! Would you like to know what was most ironic about my misadventure with radio ads? The entire time I ran them, I was also conducting a monthly game of Texas Hold 'Em with cigars. A game where entrepreneurs exchanged cards and laughs, and did thousands of dollars in business with each other. I should have spent my radio money buying boxes of cigars, cash prizes for winners, turning it into a fundraiser for nonprofits and inviting the biggest names in town.

I know of no one who does this better than Kevin Thompson, founder of the Relationship Accelerator Network. You talk about a Radically Generous Entrepreneur! Kevin now gets paid to gab on the phone with people who may as well be his childhood friends. He is the consummate relationship broker, totally selfless in promoting others and connecting them. All he asks for is a little on the back end when it works out, just like a realtor would. And he knows just how to phrase it, too. Kevin literally is a walking, talking billboard for his network. I've never had occasion to reach out to him about finding a person or group where he didn't have a connection.

Podcast Pilgrim's Progress

After I returned from New York City, I went on an interviewing rampage. The first thing I did was publish high-profile exchanges with Craig Ballantyne, Brittany Michalchuk and Paul Getter. I followed those up with some of the best connections I'd made in the mastermind. Brian Moncada, Luis Diaz and Luis Uribe all followed suit. I also dug up an old acquaintance in John Corcoran, the former Clinton White House speechwriter. Morgan Snyder soon joined, as did Rob Kosberg, who would become my next mastermind coach at Best Seller Publishing.

Not long after that, people began to come out of the woodwork. Marie Incontrera, who booked high-performance coaches and entrepreneurs from around the country, approached me. That brought Ron Carucci, Corey Blake and several others into the mix.

Once I became a client of Best Seller Publishing, I had a slew of authors to interview. Summer Peterson, Kurt Hegetschweiler and Jamie Lynn Juarez were among them. The downloads kept increasing. The audience sprang up in countries all over the world. I had people referring me guests left and right, and I started to appear on other shows as well.

At first, I was chasing audience expansion. Everyone likes to share that their show gets downloaded 100,000 times or more. There is still plenty of hype in the media today about who has the most likes, followers and so forth. And to be honest, dominant podcast names like John Lee Dumas, Joe Rogan and Dave Ramsey have much larger audiences than me. That gives them access to far more people.

What I realized, however, was that I wasn't there to build a huge following. I didn't even want a medium-

or small-sized one, according to the charts. I value my audience immensely. But it was building relationships with my *guests* that counted. You could say I was doing prospecting, sales, journalism and publicity all in one 30- to 45-minute conversation — both for myself and the guests.

The brand promise of Influencer Networking Secrets corresponds to its title. If you network with the host, who is an influencer, there are secrets. Secrets you want to know. Secret connections. Secret opportunities. Secret resources. There are secrets of how to network with influencers, and the secrets of how influencers network.

Vince Del Monte once told me this during his mastermind: "A brand is a promise repeated over and over." So with each of these guests, I would jot down notes on a pad of paper while they spoke on my show. The magic came after the recording stopped. I'd ask them if they'd welcome introductions to other hosts or guests. Sometimes, I'd know just the person they needed to speak to. It became an automatic habit. Just like I'd done during my insurance days.

Over-Deliver Like Crazy

Luis Diaz, now one of my clients, described the power behind podcast heavy hitters like John Lee Dumas and Pat Flynn. He studied the content and precision of their earliest work. In his appearance on my show, he said, "If you look at their earliest work, it's clear. They *over-delivered like crazy*." The study of their audience. The show notes. Audio quality. Everything they did was with the intent of becoming who they are today.

Luis articulated the principle of the Radically Generous Entrepreneur. I just had to find the way to my parallel version of it. I was no expert marketer of podcasts. Nor do I claim to be one today. Conversing, however, and adding value to people had always been my brand. It soon became apparent. My version of "over-delivering like crazy" on my podcast was to the *guests*.

When Aaron Walker came into the picture, I knew what to do. I just had no idea how well it would pay off.

Practical Publicity

Perhaps podcasting isn't your thing. I have some other stories to share, going back further in time. These are evergreen strategies. If you think about it long enough, you can come up with your own version of them.

Networking taught me that anyone who showed up had problems to solve. It's the nature of the beast.

We can assume the same of the business population at large. The entrepreneurial class is, after all, the problem-solving class. This puts you at an advantage, no matter your business category, as long as you don't forget whose problem you need to solve. The miracle of free market interaction comes from being obsessed with *others'* needs, not your own.

You're not reading this book because you want to get better at maintaining your equipment. You aren't looking for advice on hiring new people. We're definitely not talking about Facebook ad strategies. This is a book about <u>how to position yourself so that more people you know want to become your relational assets</u>. And when you're dealing with businesspeople, the cardinal rule of thumb is:

<u>Seek to solve the OTHER PERSON's biggest pain point</u>.

So, let's tell some stories and get down to brass tacks.

A friend owns a skilled trade business in the South. The hard part about being in any trade, construction or real estate-affiliated business is strategic partnerships. Acquiring them can be difficult, never mind keeping them. Losing them can mean a significant downturn in revenue, and more work to replace them. Let's face it … plumbers, electricians, HVAC companies, pest control — there are always plenty of them to go around. How do you set yourself apart?

In fact, let's ask a more important question: What in this day and age <u>would</u> set you apart?

It's tempting here to write simplistic equations. A + B = C. Follow three simple steps. Next thing you know, you're raking in the dough. Well, that's not how it happened for me. Some people might be able to make miracles happen in six weeks. I started my journey of learning to build relationships and communicate better many years ago, as a young man in the pre-9/11 world. I think it's a mistake to look at life and business in a linear fashion, like those charts you see representing the "ups and downs" of gross domestic product. I prefer the "ascending spiral" model, which reminds us that we all take turns being in grad school one day and kindergarten the next.

The object of my life is to become a Radically Generous Entrepreneur. Whether I do so with a financial fortune or not is quite beside the point. If you're like me, there is no other path to success of any kind because success is as much an illusion as failure. Has the Coronavirus scare not confirmed this? How do you tell the people who lost a fortune in the stock market crash and precipitous surge of unemployment claims that it was all just a dream?

I don't like to swerve off-topic here, but people sometimes read books like this hoping to find "the formula." It's not in here. It never will be. Even as I say that, however, I'm aware that there is a "formula." It takes a lot longer to work than you might want it to, but when it works, no one can stop it. Not even you.

Back to my friend with the trade business in the South. He's good at what he does. He's got maybe eight or ten competitors in a sizable city. Like any business owner, he also gets his fair share of mailers, offers and cold calls from people selling paid advertising. The temptation is to believe that the reason his phone isn't ringing is simply because no one knows he exists, and he needs to drain his bank account to build awareness.

I agree, it's bad for your marketplace not to know you exist. The trap we fall into is thinking that the answer to that problem lies (by definition) in paid advertising.

Okay ... that *might* be true! It depends on what you sell. Let's say you sell a customized t-shirt that can easily be displayed and ordered over social media. Who could blame you, if social media advertising does the trick? If you're totally dominant in your city, region or state, you need to start attracting buyers from elsewhere. That's a perfectly good reason to advertise. I encourage you to do so.

But neither of these categories suits my friend. His business is a service. He is the brand. What sets him apart is what it's like to have him service your home, versus the competition. More accurately, the brand should be "a man you can trust to look after your clients, tenants or buyers." One way to get a step ahead of waiting for someone to need your service is to make friends with people in business who already have the ear of people who need your service.

Signs and Misdemeanors

Are you starting to see how your mind should work when you think about networking? This friend could go and put signs in people's front yards. Do you read the signs your neighbors have in their yards? Especially the ones that say which security company protects them? Looking out my home office window as I write this, I notice my neighbor has a yard sign for a moving company they use. I wonder how long it's been there? (Now that I've highlighted it, you watch ... it'll be top-of-mind when my wife and I downsize after the kids leave home.)

In other words, unless you're openly advocating for a political candidate or a specific ballot initiative, signs are "white noise." Ugly lawn ornaments. (Particularly the political ones, by the way, but they at least get the attention of the passersby). Billboards, TV ads, radio ads … it's white noise to today's marketplace. Social media advertising has mitigated the problem to some extent. They at least make an effort to be granular and data-driven in which ads get served to whom. But the big networks have their limitations, especially for businesses built on personal services.

All this is to say that paid advertising has its place, for service businesses. In my opinion, that place is <u>when you have too many people in one place or niche singing your praises</u>. When you're saturated in the marketplace, and you're flush with marketing dollars. Everyone else, as Jonathan Garrick once told me, is "in the business of making or breaking relationships."

The Inside Track

I suggested that my friend start attending realtors' open houses in upscale neighborhoods. Landscapers and swimming pool contractors also make great strategic partners for him. The more of those variables he could find together in one property, the sooner he'd reach his target niche.

Once at the open house, the strategy is to "casually visit" — as though real estate was a hobby, and you're just there to see what properties are available on the market. Many people do this already. You take a walk around the property, and remark on the pool and landscaping. Ask questions, especially about what companies did such marvelous work on the outdoors. You can casually drop what business you're in if the agent asks. There's no harm in that. But don't come begging for referrals or asking to put a sign in the yard. Simply be inquisitive and respectful of the realtor's need to focus on potential buyers.

As you prepare to leave, thank the realtor for their time and ask when they'll be doing their next open house. When they tell you the date, you say something like this:

"What would you think about the idea of me coming back and doing a video to help promote your open house that day? I'd love to showcase the pool and outdoor environment, give people a reason to come check it out."

This may seem awkward at first. In fact, I'll just tell you ... it is. I'm giving you a cold-call networking scenario. If this is outside your comfort zone, you don't have to start there. Most people have a few friends already in real estate. For practice, start by going to their open houses. Go to open houses where friends and family are selling their homes. Do video tours and promote their stuff. Doing this will build up a track record on your social media profile. Later, when pitching the idea to someone you don't know very well, it'll be familiar ground for you, and much more comfortable.

This kind of selfless, supportive work ingratiates you with other entrepreneurs. Believe it or not, they're experiencing the same frustration with marketing that you are. The more I did things like this as an insurance agent, the more I got "thank you" notes. "That house sold! The one where you came and did the video tour. Thanks for your help!"

In the spiritual world, this is like "stopping to offer roadside assistance." You may not have the tow truck or gasoline, but you can definitely help signal distress. You're lending your momentum and influence to people. It creates energy, and reassures them they don't have to face their work alone. It multiplies confidence. It's how a Radically Generous Entrepreneur should think and act.

What If They Don't Have a Marketing Problem?

The day will come, especially if you do this as a habit, that you'll have a chance to promote someone who needs little to no introduction. Guests on my show like Craig Ballantyne, John Eldredge and Rabbi Daniel Lapin didn't "need" to be there. They were helping *me* by appearing. There's no shame in admitting that.

Does that mean that Craig, John and Daniel needed *nothing*? No! Quite the opposite. These people need all kinds of things. Sometimes you'll get an opportunity to provide it, but most of the time you don't. In Chapter 4, we'll discuss ways you can add value to people who don't "seem" to need it.

The entrepreneurial journey goes through stages. The first is survival, followed by success, and then significance. As long as you can identify which stage a person is in, you can eliminate the need to offer things that don't apply.

Typically, if you're meeting somebody who doesn't really need publicity, that should narrow your focus. You can certainly promote their content and websites on your personal media platform. But at this level, they are likelier to respond to requests that involve minimal effort on their part. Secondarily, they're also big on "social proof." They want client testimonials, people lending their voice to reinforce their authority. So I'm going to pull back the curtain to show you how I built the case for John Eldredge to appear on the show.

A Decade-Long Foundation

John's books first got on my radar in 2007, on a chilly desert night in Taji, Iraq. A chaplain at a service I attended offered me a copy of "Wild At Heart," John's 2001 bestseller. I read the whole book in one night; I couldn't put it down.

From there, I began to grow as a disciple in the teachings provided by John's organization, Ransomed Heart Ministries. I bought his other books. I listened to audio excerpts. I went to see him speak in 2009 at Eastside Foursquare Church in Seattle, where my in-laws attended service at the time.

After a lengthy downward spiral, I returned to the Ransomed Heart Podcast in late 2016, and signed up to go to Wild At Heart Boot Camp the following summer. By this time, they had an application for the iPhone, and John had written several more books I'd not read. I became a monthly supporter of their operation.

I knew from listening to John on the podcast that there wasn't much chance of being noticed by him. It's not because he doesn't care; he simply has too many demands on his time. You can e-mail him 1,000 times per day, it won't matter. His e-mail is kept by his team so that he only sees what he absolutely needs to see. Most high-profile influencers are like this. Even recording a great testimonial video as social proof isn't likely to break through the firewall. It might get used by the media team, but John himself might never see it. I wanted him to hear, *personally*, the passion and energy infused into my life from his work.

I started by interviewing Morgan Snyder, one of the leaders of Ransomed Heart. It took me six months from my first e-mail to the day we connected over Skype. Morgan gave a terrific interview, bolstering my confidence. In mid 2019, leveraging a good connection with Morgan's assistant, I parlayed my way into an interview with Allen Arnold. Allen is Ransomed Heart's director of content, and he also appears regularly on the podcast. I kept up an occasional correspondence with him, and connected him with several people.

All this time, I kept plugging away interviewing people with far less name recognition or notoriety. I practiced my interview style, based on Andy Stanley's methods. I kept connecting, adding and multiplying value to my guests.

Do you see where this is going? When I say that building relationships takes time, this is what I mean. People reached out to me slack-jawed when guests like John appeared on my show. "How do you do that?" they'd ask. The answer is what I call "slow-playing, with sincerity." To give without expectation of return. I could have asked Allen to connect me with John right after our interview, but at that time, I knew John wasn't looking for interviews. I was content to wait, until he WAS looking for them. Then I would strike.

Word began to spread in late 2019 that John would release his new book, *Get Your Life Back*, in February 2020. I dropped Allen a note and asked him if he had any advice for booking an interview. He did, and suggested I submit a proposal that could then be passed to John's publicity team.

Now, put yourself in John Eldredge's shoes and ask yourself if this decision requires much thought:

A new book coming out aimed at Christians, with a need to get on hundreds of shows and outlets where they're known to gather.

An offer of a friendly interview from someone steeped in Ransomed Heart culture and language, a Boot Camp alumnus and supporter.

A target client with a direct line to the target audience, currently leading a group of them through one of your books.

An interviewer with a track record of interviewing your inner circle. Two of your most prominent colleagues and friends have already appeared on this same show.

A show popular with other notable people in the Christian author/influencer space like Rabbi Lapin and Aaron Walker.

What author do you know, promoting a new book, would decline such conditions for an interview? All of John's "thinking" or deliberating was done for him. In fact, I'd be surprised if he even made the decision himself; it was likely his publicist. But in either case, how long do you think they needed to determine if it was a good fit? How many variables were left unaddressed?

This is why Pro Bono Publicity is a fundamental quality of the Radically Generous Entrepreneur. The example I give, of working my way up to John's appearance, isn't the only way to do this. But when you consider that my reach and audience size were woefully small, it left plenty of room for him to consider it a waste of time. Besides our shared faith, I had to make up the difference elsewhere.

Every prominent guest I've had on the show has come as a result of referral or recommendation from someone in their inner circle. Usually, that's because I've interviewed or added value to the inner circle members first. That's why my approach to business and attitude toward people *near* the spotlight frequently affords the chance to be *in* the spotlight.

So, if you desire the way of the Radically Generous Entrepreneur, Rule #2 is Become a Pro Bono Publicist.

CHAPTER 4 -
The Inroads

Not-For-Profit IS For-Profit

I n this chapter, I want to state my wholehearted agreement with <u>the spiritual goodness of for-profit commerce</u>. I grew up on a steady diet of slander and defamation of corporations and free enterprise. That changed in 2002 with my conversion to Christ. I couldn't help noticing how the fingers that accused and maligned capitalism were some of its wealthiest beneficiaries. They freely dined on the best of what the system had to offer, while vomiting up venom against the hand that feeds them. Hence I am and will remain an unapologetic, affectionate capitalist.

Nothing you're about to read should be interpreted to agree with the "for-profit business needs redemption" mantra. I reject that premise out of hand, especially considering its proponents' narrative. Somehow, we're led to believe nobility in work is only to be found working for nonprofits or government. Talk about institutions that make prime targets for corruption, abuse and financial malfeasance! If you can accept it, I put forward this premise: _All_ human institutions and organizations are susceptible to foul play. In each sector are authentic, heroic leaders. In each sector are slackers and opportunists.

Another quick disclosure: I'm equally adamant that participation in charitable or community causes is nothing short of a way of life for the Radically Generous Entrepreneur. You can't do this because you need a tax write-off or good publicity. (Yes, you will probably get those. But that must not govern your decision). This must flow, as my friend Dr. Andy Garrett says, purely from the joy you get from doing it. As soon as you start insisting on rewards or reciprocity for involvement, you open the door for entropy. It's important to be highly selective, and therefore highly exclusive, as to the organizations you're willing to support. You must support them from a place of authenticity, or you'll eventually burn out.

More Embarrassing Stories

A few personal stories show how I failed to understand the connection between nonprofit work and entrepreneurship. These are awkward and embarrassing, but I believe they're also helpful.

In the summer of 2014, I became president of the Olympia-Tumwater subchapter of the Association of the U.S. Army (AUSA). As I settled in, I faced an immediate need: a temporary venue for our board meeting, as our regular meeting place couldn't support us that month.

Liberty Mutual's offices were in the RE/MAX Parkside building in Tumwater. I'd struck up a casual friendship with Jim Bennett, the owner of the building. He was also the designated broker for RE/MAX Parkside, and had an office in the building. We'd frequently stop for hallway chats. I mentioned in passing one day that we needed a temporary meeting site. Jim offered the upstairs conference room. I happily accepted, as it had plenty of space with tables and chairs.

I'd been promoting AUSA wherever I went. We needed funds and awareness of our mission to support the 17th Field Artillery Brigade. There was a lot of interest for the first board meeting where I served as president. Perhaps 10 to 12 extra people joined, beyond the regulars.

It was exciting to see enthusiastic faces at this meeting. But I wasn't ready to lead at all. Some people mistook it as an invitation to a networking group. They placed business cards and flyers in front of every member present. Others were there, I'd venture, because I had a reputation for leadership and making things happen. Perhaps they were intrigued to see what we were up to.

It really didn't matter. I knew nothing about standard board meeting rules, including who could vote on motions. So when they came up for consideration, there were people saying "aye" who had no business doing so. I hadn't taken time to explain it. I knew I was in over my head, as soon as I heard the voices saying "aye." Deep inside, I sensed it but didn't know how to extricate myself or back out on what I'd agreed to.

That day represented the peak of interest in AUSA. I could feel it drop off significantly afterward. It was the beginning of an even steeper learning curve — getting people to invest time, talent and treasure in an organization where they can't reap even a financial reward. It is a hero's journey of its own — slowly, gently but enthusiastically "warming" people to the idea of sacrificing their resources to help people who can't possibly pay it back.

Motives Matter

I interviewed my friend Benjamin Case of Focused on Fundraising. His observations helped me see how little I knew about leading nonprofits.

Charitable institutions are as spiritual as their for-profit counterparts. They live and die on the same fuel. I used to think this meant money, but Ben explained it better. He said the best foundations and charities he knew had executive leaders who took pains to cast <u>vision</u>. In recruiting board members, they cast vision. In asking for funds, they cast vision. In spending and investing on beneficiaries, they still cast vision! Successful nonprofits are farmed, over time, by people who take a longer view of things.

In contrast, I spent my tenure of leadership in AUSA thinking everything was up to me. I felt I *had* to do this because I was a veteran, and because I'd volunteered. There was some nobility in my thinking, to be sure. I wanted to do what was done for me on behalf of younger veterans. But I labored under a sort of "mandatory goodness," which meant I could not scale back even if it led to nowhere. I didn't understand how to leverage the strength of others around me. So I constantly badgered the same donors, over and again, for tiny tidbits of cash or support. Not surprisingly, donors and volunteers without intrinsic motives to participate don't last long.

This isn't to say, by the way, that only a tiny handful of people on earth are capable of genuine, sincere motivation. I happen to think it's the default nature of most people. It's just that so few know how to *access* it that we resort to cheapening, coarsening tactics like over-promising on "exposure" and "community association." Somehow, we try to delude ourselves that this will lead to increases in sales. There are even donor marketing pieces that stress these "side benefits." None of it has diddly-squat to do with why people become authentic, enthusiastic supporters of nonprofits!

Therefore, these associations remain famished for new blood and cash flow. I don't recommend volunteering in executive leadership until you've been with one for a few years. You need some idea of how they work. Ben says that far too many of them will "take any volunteer willing to say 'yes.'" Once they're in, boards usually ask them to perform outside their zone of genius. You know … the outgoing, fundraising type gets assigned the duty of treasurer. The rookie PR gal suddenly becomes executive director.

Nonprofit boards frequently lack a coherent vision for raising funds. Ben said that many requests fall flat because people just go "straight to the point" and solicit funds. Without a slow, steady process of inviting donors to be part of the solution. I made that mistake dozens of times. It simply wasn't a category for me to sprinkle seed, water it, cultivate it and THEN harvest it. You would think it was, given my biblical background. I'm ashamed to say, it never occurred to me.

That didn't stop me from trying and learning, however. I labored for a further two years in the presidency of that subchapter before reaching out to Tina Torfin, in the neighboring Lacey subchapter, to merge. We were on the verge of bankruptcy and hemorrhaging volunteers; it was time to come clean, and admit I didn't know what I was doing. At the time, it felt like another compounding failure next to marital and professional difficulties. One more dagger of accusation showing how I couldn't get anything done.

Working alongside Tina gave me some fresh insights. She was much more adept at surrounding herself with good people to accomplish tasks. Her sunny disposition and warmth made it difficult to refuse a request. But she didn't run the Lacey subchapter on her own strength. That gave me my first clue; I'd failed because I'd carried too heavy a load. Moreover, as usual, I'd been in a rush to be competitive with the big local nonprofits. I was skipping over huge portions of the process.

Even More Embarrassing Stories

Around the same time, an invitation went out to parents of students at Evergreen Christian School, where my oldest son was enrolled. It was to attend the school board's meeting to hear about a proposed curriculum change. Somehow, from the way the invitation was written, I inferred an opportunity for people to volunteer to serve on the board. (It said no such thing.)

I leapt at the opportunity to be at this meeting. I wanted to meet people and get involved. If I'm honest, the greedy undertone of building connections among the gentry whose children attend the school factored into my thinking. This is painful to confess, but I've learned the power in taking ownership of my junk. I thought to myself, "Get in with Evergreen parents, and it's easy money from high-end clientele." That may be factually true, but it definitely didn't come from a place of sincerity or serenity. I was just anxious to get something going.

A friend was already serving on the board. I went to that first meeting, stayed until the end, and everything seemed hunky-dory. Then I went to a second meeting and participated in discussions through to the end. Nobody said anything directly, so I went home thinking I'd just keep at it until an opportunity presented itself.

Well, you can imagine the offense I took when I got an e-mail from the board president asking me not to return. Apparently, there'd been a communication breakdown. I honestly thought they were looking for parents to participate with the board on an ongoing basis. I was ready and willing to do it. It turned out they'd made one meeting public, to hear parental perspective on a decision. There had been no invitation to return. I was embarrassed.

I'd never been "courted" as a contributor or board member. No one ever sat me down to cast a vision. No one really knew who I was. Had someone tried that with me, I'd have been exposed. I was not a prominent, successful businessman with thousands of dollars to invest. I wasn't an experienced fundraiser or board member. I felt two inches tall reading that letter because I felt every bit the Ned Ryerson I'd ever been.

No one teaches you things like this with nonprofits. "Common sense" isn't always so common. Polite and kind as the ECS board members were, I'd set myself back further in building relationships with them. Now I would have to overcome both the hurdle of looking amateurish and find ways to make myself useful, without setting off their "phony radar," in the future.

A Ravenous Market

The 501(c)(3) "labor market" (as it were) is ravenous for meaningful relationship builders. People who embrace the nonprofit's mission, of course. But more importantly, people who know *how* to communicate their vision so that it becomes contagious. Looking back at the folly of my ECS board adventure, I'm able to see the hand of God at work, providing me with an authentic visionary avatar.

I simultaneously developed a friendship with Talia Hastie, ECS' marketing coordinator. This woman is a jewel of the Kingdom — Miss Seattle 1988 and president of the Washington Scholarship Foundation. She now serves on the board of regents for Northwest University. Talia is a <u>huge</u> relationship builder who speaks the language of exchanging value fluently. We started helping each other from our very first meeting.

Talia expertly crafted several seasonal events at ECS that raked in hundreds of thousands of dollars for the school. The routine began in the spring, at the annual "Visions" auction. I attended this several times with my wife. Talia staged an elaborate, themed "costume party" style dinner at a local golf and country club. She recruited a professional auctioneer to emcee the event. It never raised less than $100,000 in a single night. Between ticket sales, party favors, silent auction bids and the actual live auction, it was groomed to raise money. But it also gave ECS leadership the opportunity to demonstrate the power of the donations. To explain the "why" behind everything ECS does. No wonder Talia called the event "Visions."- Everyone in that room could *see* concrete reasons that their donations mattered.

If we're willing to proceed slowly, we can understand what makes this work. Talia commands tremendous participation and financial commitment from donors. There IS a place for the for-profit entrepreneur in all of this. I joined Talia's procurement committee for just that reason. It was one area where I knew I could make myself useful. As each fundraiser came around, I was able to get donations, gift certificates and prizes.

I also sat in on several meetings. I disliked my short, to-the-point way of communicating when I watched Talia. She was a million times better at schmoozing than I was. True, she has a vivacious and effervescent personality. She was never in a rush, always content in the present moment. She was busier than I was, but she seemed to have more time than I did. She didn't know any magic spells, or use strong-arm persuasion tactics. What she had more than anything was *authenticity*.

That is what leads me to conclude that to truly partner with a charitable or community cause, we have a Kingdom job ahead of us. We must not only become the kind of person who can occupy such a position; we also have to be very discerning in our choice of cause. We must have full knowledge of our limitations, so we don't carry the world on our shoulders. We must renounce greed and lust, and not let them into our motives for participating. (I did none of this in the stories I mention, by the way.)

Let Business Take the Lead

I interviewed my friend and accountability partner Cameron Hall in the spring of 2019. We'd both walked away from Vince Del Monte's mastermind. Neither of us could afford the cost, even though there was a ton of value. One reason we both felt discouraged was we were both rookies in rooms full of online millionaires. It was easy to feel "out of your league."

The reason I wanted to interview Cam was because of something he said during one of our calls. We'd been talking about volunteer work. I mentioned how valuable it had been, in my early days in insurance. By volunteering, I'd learned a "shortcut" to encounter other professionals in a setting that avoided the "for profit" environment of networking groups. The authenticity of the conversations I had at these events always stuck with me. There had to be something to it.

Cam provided the missing clue. He said mastermind leaders should provide organic opportunities for members to decompress and process what they learn. The pace was too intense, too frenetic for rookies. Shared work on behalf of the less fortunate creates an ideal environment for those conversations to take place organically. Putting these together gave us an idea for a unique mastermind approach.

I first volunteered in the community back during my earliest days at Liberty. I got recruited by Jackie Ashley, then serving as president of Rebuilding Together Thurston County. We got assigned a repair job on a home in the declining town of Rainier, Wash. Our work for the day was to help with yard and exterior maintenance for an aging World War II veteran and his wife, who couldn't afford repairs the home needed.

I lugged my personal gardening tools, shovels, weed eater and old pickup truck down to their home. It was tidy, as you'd expect from that generation, but clearly falling into disrepair. Our group of loan officers, insurance agents, contractors and realtors spread out over the property. I did weed eating until the call went out for some fresh gravel in the driveway. The elderly husband was confined to a go-kart, like you'd see for disabled customers in grocery stores. We needed to smooth out the space between the ramp leading up to their deck and the driveway with gravel so he could drive on and off. I'd brought a cubic yard of gravel.

Then, I spent the rest of the time shoveling gravel out of the back of my truck, which "paved the way" for some great conversations with other men who helped me. You can imagine, as an Iraq veteran, the privilege and honor I felt at helping one of my combat forebears. The old man shook my hand and said, "Thank you."

I replied, "No, no. Thank *you*. Thanks to you I grew up speaking English instead of German."

The Payoff

Participating in that work fomented the free exchange of information and value. It came through casual conversations done over simple tasks, with no expectation of pay or reward. It helped me drop the salesman facade and focus on the humanity of people I worked with. I discerned a non-financial reward from the same effort — a sincere attempt to care for the needs of another of God's children.

Ongoing partnership with nonprofits could give younger, more inexperienced entrepreneurs a chance to learn about how they work. That way, dummies like Paul Edwards wouldn't walk into board meetings acting like they own the place. By engaging with a local group to dig ditches, fill bags of food or pick up trash, you foster shared experiences.

Business is a mental sport, as my mentor Dan Lok observed. So entrepreneurs should relax and recreate with <u>physical</u> tasks instead of mental ones. My pastor, Jon Cobler, offered a corresponding quote that goes, "If you earn a living with your hands, you should relax by working with your head. But if you earn a living with your head, you should relax by working with your hands."

So Cam and I hatched the idea of a "volunteer day" built into a mastermind meeting. On this day, all members would be asked to leave electronic devices behind. They'd have to bring a change of work clothes, and prepare for a day of getting dirty. The only benefit they'd receive is the sheer joy of putting smiles on others' faces. But naturally, through working alongside their fellow members, they'd have more meaningful, longer-lasting conversations. As I learned early on, I sold more insurance shoveling gravel and trimming weeds than I did pontificating about coverage rates.

Camaraderie multiplies when you get Radically Generous Entrepreneurs working together. They will stick with a group's mission long after everyone else has disappeared, and they won't walk away or disappear without at least fulfilling their commitments and trying to pass on what they've learned. When you meet such a person, their objective will never devolve from the nonprofit's agenda into their own private business one. I recommend this, particularly if you're facilitating a mastermind. Insist on it as a condition of membership.

Be Willing to Do the "Dirty Work"

I was pleasantly surprised how easily business took place when I showed up for nonprofit work. It completely bypassed sales conversations. Often, people would ask me for insurance quotes simply because I was the only person they knew who provided them. My character — and in some cases, even my expertise — needed no further demonstration.

My relationship with my biggest insurance client comes to mind. In 2015, I was in a circle of people at the Lewis County Business Showcase in Chehalis, Wash. The topic was public speaking, and of perhaps10 people taking turns sharing their feelings, I was the only one to say, "I love public speaking."

Melinda Wilkes, who organized the event, stood next to me. She immediately grabbed me by the arm and said, "Good, I'm glad you like public speaking because you can finish doing the raffle prizes for me." Within moments, I was in my element, standing on the stage and raffling off prizes in my radio announcer voice. I now had 10 times the eyes and ears on me as I'd had 20 minutes earlier, and everyone knew who I was. (This is one way you scale networking).

I wouldn't equate public speaking with the outdoor work I mentioned earlier. But most people are more eager to pull weeds than speak to a room full of strangers. So that's the "dirty work" analogy. Perhaps it's better said, "Do the work no one else is willing or eager to do."

Three weeks later, Melinda sent me a note asking if I'd be open to emceeing the Miss Lewis County Pageant. I had zero familiarity with the Miss America program, but I accepted without hesitation. I knew enough to know that willingness to provide for one need would give me opportunity to provide for another.

I also knew I'd get more opportunities to connect with more people. I'd gone from an audience of 10 (the public speaking circle) to an audience of 40-50 (the business showcase), and now I'd host an audience of several hundred people (the pageant). Complete with tuxedoed Bond photos surrounded by beautiful pageant contestants (publicity). You see how this works?

The second year I played this role, my co-hostess was Samantha Styger. Sam is an executive vice president of the Line-X Corporation and co-owner of the Twin Cities Line-X franchise in Centralia. She learned of my occupation right as her former agent went out of business. Over the next nine months, she moved a massive $100,000-premium empire under my care. Sam became, dollar for dollar, the most valuable client I had during my six years in the business.

Holding the Position

Now, let's say you hold the office of president of the board, or any outreach position, such as public relations or fundraising. At this point, according to Ben Case, <u>vision</u> must become the core of everything. One by one, with every opportunity, you need to speak into existence what you presently cannot see.

Aaron Walker told the story of one of his pastors at the church he attends in Nashville. He said this man built a church of perhaps 600 people into a colossal 7,000-member megachurch. To do this, he sat patiently through one personal meeting after another with board members, staff, lay leadership, and — most importantly — regular congregants! Over the course of several months, he kept laying out vision. The congregants agreed. They liked his ideas. They added their input.

When the pastor would introduce new parts of the vision publicly, he won overwhelming support. Many congregants thought he was adopting *their* ideas, and in some cases, they were right! This man didn't care who got the credit, however. He understood that when you have a body of committed believers roaring their agreement with your agenda, the organization grows very quickly and more get added to your number daily.

Right as I heard Aaron tell this story, I realized part of the reason for the growth of the young men's life group I lead. I make time to meet each young man for coffee or lunch. To listen to what's on their mind. To reflect their lives back to them, and understand them on a deeper level. I get the chance to describe my vision. It resonates with them. They participate eagerly.

Ben taught me to look at several criteria to consider serving in a nonprofit. How does their mission "sync" with your personal and professional vision? How well do they partner with the for-profit world? How well do they create opportunities for people to experience and wield their culture? How selective are they with people who volunteer? Is there consistent turnover, so that leadership doesn't become stale? Is there ongoing training for people to pursue leadership positions? Do they refrain from burdening volunteers with duties they aren't qualified to perform?

This rules out most nonprofits, but I think many nonprofits rule themselves out by shortcutting the importance of thinking deeply about these questions. There's frankly a lot more to succeeding as a nonprofit than simply having a board and a cause celebre. This is what I learned on the journey I took to discover that Not-For-Profit IS For-Profit. People's charitable and community causes are *inroads* for you to deepen relationships.

Epilogue at Evergreen Christian School
Now back to ECS, where as a novice networker, I'd made a fool of myself by self-nomination to the school board without their vote. Or the people's vote. Or anyone's vote, for that matter. The only person I consulted was myself.

Talia gave me a shot to speak at the school's 2014 Veterans' Day Assembly. I leveraged my role at AUSA to procure an honor guard from Joint Base Lewis-McChord. I made a slideshow with photos from Iraq and gave a talk to students about being deployed to the Middle East.

The event also produced some professional photos. One captured me looking like a pastor, at the lectern, on a well-lit stage in business attire. Posting that picture to Facebook clued me in to the value of professional photography as a means of self-promotion. Do you see the value that you reap when you volunteer to do things like this?

During this process, I learned Talia was trying to procure a tablet or iPad for the spring Visions Auction. This made me think of Jessica Lugo, a friend of mine working for Dell's Military Program. They had a division assigned to reaching the local business community. I scheduled a meeting between the two.

The meeting went well. Not only did Dell donate a tablet, but Talia also invited them to bid on a deal to replace substantial portions of the school's aging technology. This saved the school at least $10,000 in projected expenses. Another entrepreneur I know, Matt Purcell, donated a free pest control inspection from his company, PCI Pest Control. Matt ended up doing some work for Talia, and got connected to several other Evergreen parents.

On Talia's introduction, I developed a casual friendship with Jim Ladd, the senior pastor of Evergreen Christian Community (the school's adjacent, overseeing church). For the launch of my first book he recorded a 60-second video testimonial for the book, in which he said:

"I've seen Paul demonstrate the power of his principles and live them out. They turn out to be very compatible with my faith system and the teachings of Jesus. One of them is this broad, simple idea that when you exist to serve others and give rather than take, and when your pour out your life, <u>you just can't out-give or out-produce the return on it.</u> The secret is to give your life to others, investing and adding value to them. Paul gives very specific ways to do that, which bring value to people's lives and businesses, and come full circle back to your own."

If your phone isn't ringing and your numbers aren't where they need to be, get out of the office. Reconnect with your best allies, find out what community projects they're working on. Get on the phone to your network. Make things happen for them. Then sit back and watch as God returns the favor and makes things work for you.

CHAPTER FIVE -
Owning It

How to Network with Dream Connections

One day, I plan to write a book about my experience based around this Proverb: "*A lizard can be caught with the hand, yet it is found in kings' palaces.*" (Proverbs 30:28) There's scarcely a more apt description of my life. (I was thinking of calling it "The Lizard King," but I have a feeling I might get a letter from the lawyer for Jim Morrison's estate.)

I've waited a long time to write this chapter from the perspective I have today. It takes a lot of trial and error to become a pro relationship builder. You might have to go through a thousand people to find <u>the one</u> who shatters the invisible barrier. That's how it happened for me. You might have it easier or more difficult. I choose not to speak outside my own experience.

Like building a business, you reach a tipping point in building connections. You get smarter about who actually cares. You remain polite and helpful to everyone. But you get wiser about who you *invest* in. You spend more time on fewer people. The time you spend receives so much attention that it can't help but pay off.

Then, one day, in the twinkling of an eye … everything changes.

The Training Grounds

I felt encouraged in my early days connecting with local, influential people. In Olympia, I became something of a "local insurance agent for celebrities." I didn't hold all of the biggest accounts, but I got several key community leaders. It was enough to get myself invited to many gatherings and occasions that were, otherwise, restricted or off limits.

In the fall of 2015, planning began for two key non-profit events. I took the lead in converting our monthly game of poker and cigars into a fundraiser for the Association of the U.S. Army. On the pageant side, we were coordinating judges and sponsors for the 2016 Miss Thurston County event. The connection I saw between these two was John Setterstrom, the CEO of the Lucky Eagle Casino in Rochester, Wash. We needed a smoke-friendly venue for the poker game and a celebrity judge for the pageant. John would do fine for both.

One doesn't simply e-mail an executive of John's level and ask him for these things. While he wasn't a global celebrity, I couldn't just pop down to the casino and waltz into his office for a chat. I needed an inside loop to get in front of him for any length of time. I had one, probably 30 to 60 seconds in duration. My friend Cameron Wilson, a commercial realtor who played in the poker game, knew where I could meet John. He invited me to join a small, private fundraiser gathering for gubernatorial candidate Bill Bryant. I happily accepted.

Be An Angler

The first principle of networking with high-profile people is to "Be An Angler." As any good bodybuilder knows, the way to make muscles grow is to attack them from multiple angles. You don't reflexively train them the same way each time. Differentiating the attack forces new scar tissue in different parts of the muscle. This is what adds mass and volume, so the muscles begin to "snake" beneath the skin, creating a defined, lean appearance.

John Setterstrom wasn't going to this fundraiser to transact business, but he was going there *for business reasons*. That's my favorite way to describe proper orientation in networking. If I show up somewhere, I'm there for business reasons. I don't go to hand out cards or sell my services. But I *do* go to meet people, to be generous, to educate and help people think.

Viewed from this angle, it would've made no sense for me to walk up to John and ask if we could use the

Lucky Eagle for the poker game. He had no idea who I was. I could easily arouse suspicion because my business card would give away that I was an insurance salesman. That left only one option: I had to lead with inviting John to be a celebrity judge for Miss Thurston County.

John's face broke into a wide smile when I walked up and introduced myself that way. "My name's Paul Edwards. You don't know me, but I've been looking to meet you because I'm on the board of the Miss Thurston County Pageant. We're looking for celebrity judges, and your name came up."

"That sounds fun," John said. "Here's my card. Send me an e-mail. I *will* reply to you."

I could hardly believe it. A stone-cold introduction morphed, in 30 seconds of interaction, into a warm source of support. It's true, John was known for community benevolence. He is a Kingdom believer ... in executive leadership of a casino. To him, the only logical way to mitigate the perception of "vice" for the casino was to be extravagantly generous. So I won't go so far as to say that he was a "hard target." But he was an extremely busy man who would have dodged any other angle. I'd picked the right one. I didn't breathe a word about AUSA. I definitely didn't even *think* about insurance.

Corresponding with John to get him confirmed as a judge gave me the opportunity to ask his support elsewhere. We procured a private room with card dealers for the AUSA Poker Game. We raised $4,000 in one evening from that game. John and I kept up a good relationship, including after he stepped down from the casino. It's one of the finest stories I have from my days of training to network with a dream connection.

Keep Your Ear to the Ground

Another move that paid off handsomely was the relationship I built with Andy Ryder. He owns the Shur-Kleen Car Wash franchise and serves as mayor of Lacey, Wash.

We got acquainted by encounters at community events in and around Lacey. Our exchanges gave me plenty of perspective on how little "free time" civic leaders have. Even with a business that involves very little on-site "work" from its owner. Even as a weak-executive mayor of a medium-sized town. Andy, I discovered, would kill for 30 minutes to himself, where nobody asks for anything or needs his input.

All you have to do is take a look at your own life in the 21st century. You can easily get an idea of the busyness level for influencers, celebrities and politicians. Maybe the Coronavirus scare gave us a little break. But if you think about it, the pace of life gives you an advantage for the moment you get in front of people like Andy. If you're willing to Keep Your Ear to the Ground, you'll get your chance.

Needless to say, we're not talking here of your "chance" to pitch your product. We're talking about your chance to give them a safe haven. To find them a small corner of their world where there's no media, crowds, meetings, ribbon-cuttings, town halls, mandatory photo shoots or speeches. Just them, and something fun or relaxing to do ... and you. Andy occasionally played in the monthly poker/cigar game. He knew I had a reputation for traditional, masculine "fun" and giving guys a chance to relax. So my next move was a natural one.

A firearms enthusiast and owner of multiple guns, Andy didn't know I was a member at an indoor shooting range called Glacier Gun Club. Glacier was a novelty in Olympia in those days, and many prominent businessmen held memberships there. It turned out to be the "silver bullet" that "triggered" our business relationship.

One day, Andy showed up at Ricardo's Restaurant, owned by our mutual friend Rick Nelsen (another of my "celebrity clients"). I regularly met there Fridays for lunch with a loose affiliation of Rick's friends. Andy joined us on this occasion, and we got to chatting about guns. I mentioned my membership at Glacier. He said, "I've wanted to go down and try that place for a while. I just can't be bothered to go through the hassle of signing up for a membership."

Bingo.

"No worries," I said. "I've got guest passes. I can get you in. All you need to do is bring your heat. After we put some rounds downrange, they have a cigar lounge in the back. We can sit back there and chew the fat if you want." And just like that, I had a two-hour private meeting with a wealthy, influential, powerful political leader.

Do you see how this works? Prominent people are starved for simple, ordinary experiences that require little to nothing of them. This is why they employ executive assistants and "handlers." There isn't the bandwidth in any single human being to do much beyond what they already do. Not to mention the mixed reaction they get from the public every time they bat an eyelid. I'm convinced that, among other things, Andy saw an opportunity to "disappear" and simply be himself.

So off we went to Glacier Gun Club, where we fired off a bunch of rounds. We smoked cigars and chewed the fat, in Glacier's upscale "speakeasy" settings. Yes ... we even talked about insurance! Eventually, Andy became a client. I was working on acquiring his entire portfolio when I was fired from Insurance Services Group.

Done-For-You Publicity

During his appearance on my podcast, Vince Del Monte joked, "You're my No. 1 unpaid promoter, Paul." I'm quite certain it was exaggerated. Or at the very least, I've long since been surpassed. I joked back, "You'll get my bill in the mail, Vince."

But there was a season, under Vince's nutrition and exercise programs, that I did my best to give him a lot of reinforcement. I led several people to try them. I talked about it constantly on social media. The proof was there for everyone to see. I went from 26.5% body fat to 11.7% in six months. It was my biggest personal accomplishment in years. Unwittingly, I was following half a dozen key practices for worming my way into the consciousness of an influencer.

I came into Vince's Facebook group, Team Del Monte, with a pre-existing skill for promoting others. So I started uploading progress pics and encouraging other members. As the fat melted and I became lean and muscular, I started sharing progress photos. I'd never been able to display muscle in my life. I constantly gave Vince the credit. The more I succeeded with one program, the quicker I moved to purchase others in his product suite.

Vince was migrating away from selling fitness products and information at the time. He wanted to coach other fitness business owners. He'd started his own high-end mastermind. It took a while, but I persuaded my wife that I should join it. I didn't last very long, as I didn't have the funds to support it. But I made two trips to Toronto and New York City to attend mastermind meetings where I met incredible people of great character and caliber. If I could have afforded to remain there, I wouldn't have thought twice.

As you can imagine, this huge change prompted handwritten notes of appreciation. I was used to doing that for my insurance clients. I later interviewed Vince and his father, Luciano, for my podcast. I connected him with other hosts I knew, such as Marc Mawhinney, to give him even more exposure. Most of this simply flowed from what I was used to doing. But then I stumbled across an interesting article that put it all in one box.

Funnily enough, the man who wrote the article also appeared on my podcast — John Corcoran, a former Clinton White House speechwriter. John had parlayed his gift with networking all the way to the highest levels of government. He now runs a company called Rise25. They provide done-for-you podcasting and event coordination services. But this business arose from his original one, The Smart Business Revolution, which is where I found this article.

John listed seven things you could do to build relationships with high performers:

- Record a video of yourself reviewing their product or book
- Ask for an interview
- "Buy" some of their time
- Meet at a conference
- Reach out using a heartfelt letter
- Look for mutual friends
- Honor them with an award

That list actually gave me the idea for this book — to define and organize a blueprint of how I network! John's approach was systematic. I'd followed his list without really knowing it. But Vince's feedback confirmed I was practicing the way of the Radically Generous Entrepreneur.

Ask the Three Big Questions

Learning these questions from Vince gave me an evergreen strategy of icebreakers.

- What's going well for you lately?
- What's not going so well for you?
- What are you looking forward to?

I hope the difference is clear. This is not like asking generic, hackneyed questions like "What's new?" These questions dig deeper beneath the surface, but they're not rude or imposing. They're healthful, pot-stirring questions that make people's brains move.

They also have a myriad of rephrasings and "alternates" you can use, depending on the person. Recently, I asked it this way. "What's the best part of being you right now?" Another time, to one of my pastors, I asked, "What's the hardest part of your job?" Don't feel like you have to use word-for-word recitals of these questions. They just help you understand what people really want to talk about. If you can keep it in mind to ask them, you'll soon find yourself in the same captivating place of a devoted, attentive listener.

I'll never forget the first time I tried using these questions. I was at a networking group in Olympia, run by my friend Alan Shimamoto. Alan picked up on the importance of giving people "socializing time." Everybody gets a turn to speak, according to a timer. But I got bored of trying to come up with something "new" every time. If you're consistent enough at the same group, the regulars start to have a good idea of what you're up to. And if you sell insurance, as I did, there's a good bet they're not in a rush to find out.

I decided to turn the tables on this. I ceded my talk time. "Instead of me yammering about myself for three or four minutes," I said, "why don't each of you take a turn to answer a question I'll pose?" They agreed. One question at a time, I threw them out. And the responses I got <u>flooded</u> the table with conversation. Suddenly, each person was getting high-fives and recognition for good things. They found resources and empathy for challenges. They got moments to highlight future opportunities. And I got to be the instigator, setting myself apart from the self-oriented talk that normally dominated the table.

Ever since Vince shared these questions, I've not found a scenario where they haven't worked. (To be fair, I've not tried them at funerals. That might be an exception. Please don't try it and then blame me ...)

These questions also work on high performers and socially prominent people. If you're caught off guard, unprepared to meet them, they're a great fallback plan. It's a bit like an "interview on the spot." If you haven't got an angle and there's no time for groundwork in the other categories I've mentioned, then this is your starting point.

If it *does* become your starting point, the second question is usually where you'll find the gold. Busy executives, politicians and celebrity-influencers have difficulties and desires too. The fact that they're raking in dough is irrelevant. It's the human condition to ask, "What's next?" And you can be sure they're asking.

As an example, Rabbi Daniel Lapin appeared on my show in August 2019. I devour his content. On one episode, he shared content from an article written by Camille Paglia, the noted feminist commentator. He casually added that he'd very much like to meet her.

It would be presumptuous to think Rabbi Lapin is incapable of contacting Ms. Paglia on his own. They're both influential members of the American media. It wouldn't surprise me to learn that he's already tried to communicate with her. That's irrelevant; I want you to pay attention to *how my mind works* when someone discloses information like this.

Immediately, I thought of John Corcoran. Was there a chance he knew her? She comments on social and political issues. He once wrote speeches for President Bill Clinton and California Governor Gray Davis. I could at least make the attempt. I did; John wrote back to say he didn't know her.

But that was probably my 300th "practice round" of trying to facilitate connections. It works all the time with people you've never heard of. The bigger they are, the more awkward it can be, and the less frequently you get the shot. But if you don't take the shot, as Wayne Gretzky said, you'll miss it one hundred percent of the time. Just be sure to keep an eye on when and where that influential person will next appear. You may need to go to their next speech or meet-and-greet to follow up.

In the meantime, there were other connections to be made. By joining the Iron Sharpens Iron mastermind, I met Derek Champagne, founder of a marketing firm called The Artist Evolution. In his spare time, Derek cultivates relationships with current, retiring and former professional athletes. He's building a mastermind to allow these athletes to connect and grow personally and professionally.

Naturally, my existing relationships made sense. Retired Indianapolis Colts lineman Shawn Harper and Milwaukee Brewers first baseman Lyle Overbay were both God-fearing men I could refer. Learn to keep a good Inventory of Relational Assets, as Brian McRae says. You'll have fewer conversations where you don't have something to contribute.

Focus on the Farm Team

Advanced networking is like any other professional skill. The law of 10,000 hours applies. The more you do it, the more of it you get. The more practice reps you take, the fewer mistakes you make. That's why you can't wait <u>until</u> you get a "dream connection" moment. You have to start with the ordinary people you meet every day.

In the insurance business, this was my custom. As I transitioned to entrepreneurship, it became a force of nature all its own. I believe it keeps expanding because I keep doing it at the simplest, most fundamental levels.

Speaking of pro athletes like Shawn and Lyle, do you know what they did every off-season? They went straight back to the basics. Boring, fundamental work that consumes hours. One single move in games that involve *thousands* of moves. Thousands of swings of the bat. Thousands of snaps and adjusting to audibles. These men practiced the same move more times in one day than the average person inhales and exhales.

I do no less with networking. In talking to a young lady at church, I discovered she had an interest in learning about the private security and protection business. Now, which former football player did I just mention who also owns a private security firm? That's right. Shawn Harper owns one. I called in the favor and connected them.

The young men in our church's Young Adults ministry are used to this. I raid my bookshelf to make room for new stuff to read by giving the books I've read to them. I introduce them to people who are hiring for jobs. I connect them with potential opportunities. It's *how more businessmen should be*, if you ask me. It isn't really a skill, but it <u>seems</u> like one because so few people do it.

After interviewing John Eldredge, I got a ton of support from some great Kingdom allies. Pastor Tommy Miller of Legacy Church, Patrick Antonucci of Dad Hackers and Pastor Chase Merrell, on staff at our church, all trumpeted their applause. They all got introductions to book John on their shows.

This reminds me of something I heard from Jayson Gaignard. He said, "If you give enough people a hand on their way up, you'll find plenty of hands reaching out to catch you when you fall." This is true, as I'd witnessed when I left the insurance business.

Here's another question to ask yourself, in the event you break through and become wealthy and influential. Will you remember the people who took a chance on you back when no one else would? Or will you let the sycophants get to your head? You could one day be in a place where, like Andy Ryder, you dream of five minutes of privacy. On that day, the people you'll remember the most are the ones who supported you before you won widespread acclaim.

There are ample ways to focus on the farm team. I've done a ton of podcast interviews with people you've never heard of. Everyone in business benefits from more exposure rather than less. I spend a lot of time making personal introductions — free bookings, free inroads, free publicity. I considered turning it into a brokerage of strategic partnerships like Kevin Thompson does. But that changed when my relationship with Aaron began to grow.

A Dream Realized

Aaron Walker first came to me by recommendation from Patrick Antonucci. I knew he'd make a good guest because I was trying to build my own mastermind at the time. As the leader of the Iron Sharpens Iron mastermind, Aaron scaled the concept. He leads 15 groups of 8 to 12 men each. It's now branching into versions for women and young men 20-25.

Aaron also brought some degree of notoriety as a friend of celebrated Christian authors like Dan Miller and Dave Ramsey. My wife and I are two-time graduates of Dave's Financial Peace University program. We'd also read Dan's book, "48 Days to the Work You Love."

We had a great conversation on our first interview. On the post-interview chat, Aaron said something that carried a ton of weight. Have you ever had that happen? Somebody says an ordinary sentence, but it sounds like a royal proclamation?

"I want to build a relationship with you." It wasn't a phrase I'd never heard before. It was just the first time I'd believed it when someone said it. I could tell he wasn't trying to sell me. He didn't need anything from me. There was utter sincerity in his voice.

Over the following six months, I did what I normally do with guests. I connected Aaron with other podcasters looking for guests. I connected him with my best friend, Dave Culbreath, who lives near him in Nashville. I brought him bookings and some prospects for a product he was about to launch: The Mastermind Playbook.

That playbook also provided a convenient excuse for me to invite Aaron back on the show. Again, we had a great interview. But this time, the post-interview chat led to a life-changing moment.

"Paul," he said, "you have helped me so much by introducing me to all these great people. You need to un-humble yourself for a moment and tell me something I can do for you."

Aaron knew that my attempt to start my own business wasn't getting traction. By this point, I was in the habit of confessing it to anyone who asked. As we dug a little deeper, he asked me what kind of skills I could bring to an organization like his.

It occurred to me that Aaron didn't need my help leading masterminds. That left only public speaking, which he also didn't need, and writing. I'd never attempted to earn a living from writing. It had always seemed like something out of my reach. Even though, by this time, I was a bestselling author, I'd not made more than maybe $200 in book sales.

We settled on experimenting with me as a content ghostwriter for Aaron's company, View From the Top. He needed a pair of weekly blogs, daily Alexa brief scripts and micro-content (snippets and tweets). I agreed to do it to give him a chance to "test drive" a business relationship.

I can't say for certain that there's any experience, background or natural inclination that made it work. All I can say is I had three advantages. I was a like-minded Christian entrepreneur. I was a product of masterminds. And I have the same heart for younger men that Aaron does. Packaged into 30 years of creative writing experience, I suddenly had a spark of hope. A light at the end of a 17-month tunnel of zilch.

In no time, Aaron's content output began to churn like a well-oiled machine. He was back to releasing weekly blogs, Alexa brief episodes and micro-content. The comments began to crackle on his e-mail.

The resurgence caught the attention of several people. One was Brian McRae, the head of Mastermind St. Louis. He called me at the end of 2019 to talk; he needed help similar to what I did for Aaron.

One week later, I had my second client.

Aaron was so excited to learn this news that he went on an e-mail rampage. He wrote to a ton of other influencers, thought leaders and executives he knew. I found myself in serious business conversations with people who needed and could afford my services. I added four more clients over the next several weeks. The drought is over. But more importantly, the concepts of this book came true. I had "networked" my way into my own ghostwriting business.

The power of relational capital can't be overstated. I finally saw it come to fruition. Jesus taught us to "use worldly wealth to gain friends for yourselves, so that when it's gone, you'll be welcomed into eternal dwellings" (Luke 16:9).

The "Lizard King" had finally escaped being caught with the hand. I'd begun to live in kings' palaces.

CHAPTER SIX -
Frequency

Persuasion in Print

You'd think this is an easy chapter for a professional writer. That's the great irony of my business: words fail at the strangest of turns.

Stories are more reliable, especially in the 21st century. In the first two versions of this book, I had a handful of stories to share. Now, I have a catalog of them saved in my e-mail. I created a folder called "Connections," which contains hundreds of messages exchanged with my network. I am usually (but not always) the initiator in the threads.

The "stories" of these e-mails usually summarize the backgrounds of people I introduce. But I believe people *themselves* are stories — living, breathing ones. Through these messages, I've had a hand in writing new chapters for people. Some of them have gone further than I could have imagined. Bringing together two living stories that find synergy unleashes spiritual power you don't know existed. But it sure is fun to watch.

I learned to introduce people via e-mail from Craig Ballantyne. He shared a template he uses. I hope he won't sue if I reprint the gist of it here:

Dear {NAME},

I want to introduce you to someone you should know ... my friend, Craig Ballantyne. He's the bestselling author of The Perfect Day Formula and a high performance business coach.

Craig coaches entrepreneurs and professionals to maximize their time and productivity. He has helped me straighten out so many kinks in my personal and professional life. I know he could help you do the same.

Craig, I want you to meet Paul Edwards, bestselling author of "Business Beyond Business" and a top-rate freelance ghostwriter.

Paul captures your voice in print, and produces quality content tailored to your audience so you can churn it out like a machine. He's helped me ratchet up engagement from my followers big time. I know he could help you do the same.

I strongly recommend the two of you get on a phone call together. You'll both get a lot out of it.

I'll let you take it from here.
{SIGNED}
PS - I know both of you would be happy to send each other free copies of your bestselling books. Just swap the best shipping addresses.

I started using this technique for introductions, changing the names and tailoring it according to the situation. It produced exactly the response I wanted, nearly every time I used it. What people do with it afterward is secondary in importance. What matters is the memorability of the gesture, and the response rate. If you want an e-mail that people are inclined to open, use something like this one.

You could say this is my print version of Vince Del Monte's "three big questions." People hardly ever ignore it, or have nothing to say. It's funny when you hear people talk about "limiting e-mails to five sentences or less." This particular message has quite a bit to say, and I've never had to shorten it. It's just so well-worded, you don't want to stop reading it. Some people in my network receive it regularly, and they're accustomed to it. They know exactly which sentences to highlight for information I share about the other person. A few of them have started using it.

When you encounter a message like this, there's a good bet you're dealing with a Radically Generous Entrepreneur. It's common for them to be <u>persuasive in print</u>.

Sell Me This Print

By "persuasive," I don't necessarily mean "copywriting that earns money." That's certainly one way to persuade, but it's hardly the only one. It can have a variety of meanings. Everything from communicating sincerity to withholding information when disclosing it would be foolish. What matters is obsession with what gets received on the other end of the line. If you think of the definition of the word "persuade," its practical outcome is that the receiving party begins to think and behave in a like or corresponding manner. This is most likely to occur when you are obsessed with the finer details of the message.

Here's a fascinating side note: Most people understand this rule for verbal, in-person communication. Most have decent degrees of intuition about people around us. We can read body language, perceive intonation and sense the warmth or chill of an interaction. It only takes a brief, uncomfortable pause in dialogue for anxiety about another person's reaction to seep in. Yet for that same majority of people, that goes out the window when we sit at the keyboard.

Now, I don't mean here that we turn into "keyboard warriors" of online political debates or Reddit forums. I simply mean we take nothing like the care in print that we do in person. We aren't exactly taught how to do it, and the truth is most people who "should" know how it's done have no idea. So, we're polite and thoughtful enough not to be rude or obnoxious in our messages. But we remain woefully ignorant of tension the written word can create. Or fail to create.

Recall the quote I referenced from Jesus on this subject: "Be wise as serpents and harmless as doves" (Matthew 10:16). Let me tell you why I think this passage has as much to do with written communication as it does in-person.

As we observed, serpents have poor audio and visual acuity. They can't see to save their lives. They don't have ears. They survive on their ability to perceive prey through heat signatures. This is why snakes appear to move slowly, watchful and observantly, toward their prey. They don't *rush* at them like a charging lion. Nor do they snare them, like a Venus flytrap. They must make a move, but they can't afford to make the wrong one. So they "inch" toward the target, carefully reviewing and processing the circumstances.

To write like a Radically Generous Entrepreneur, you must place a premium on the "heat signature" of messages you send. You must not "rush" people in your writing, nor can you ignore the degree of pre-existing "warmth" you may already have. Don't vomit all kinds of information all over them, assuming you have more of a bond than you actually do. Neither should you be cold and merciless like a Venus flytrap, unresponsive to outreach. You're looking for the spiritual "comfort zone," and sometimes you're trying to find it with strangers. And that's not easily done, particularly if you sense the moment has come to insist on another means of communication.

When I Don't Communicate in Print

Until now, I've described how I communicate when I'm the initiator. But many introverted people reading just said, "Fine and dandy. What about when you are the <u>recipient</u> of the message that's awkward to answer in print?"

To which I reply, I have another story.

I remember an occasion where two friends in business took a dislike toward each other. There was some bad chemistry. It started to get quite nasty, and I was very embarrassed. I'd invited them both to an event I hosted, and their disagreement made it an unpleasant task. It's "no man's land" for a connector to bring together people who end up hostile with each other.

One of them texted me afterward to try and win me to his side of the disagreement. It was uncomfortable. I tried, without much luck, to present a wider view of my neutrality. But I could sense that he was getting more wound up. So I wrote, "I don't think we should have this conversation by text. Let's meet for coffee and hash it out."

We never pursued the matter further. I'm glad we didn't; I doubt I'd have done much better in person than I did on text. But it cued me into something powerful about our spiritual nature in the written form. Maybe you'd agree: significant parts of our tone, body language and emotional state get amplified (or obscured) by print.

Some people type "Ok" and just mean, "Ok." Others do it to avoid conflict, like I did with my insurance boss. And others do it when they'd really like to blow a stack and crash into you like a wrecking ball. We subject our communication to the fog and confusion of interpretation. Add in the timing of the message, and it can mean different things on different days. Would you agree?

One day you really mean, "Ok." Another day you're frustrated, tired and impatient … and what you really mean should not be spoken or printed.

And there's a flipside. Excitable, extroverted people can overwhelm, for better or worse. People who are big on cheerleading and encouraging others can start to ring hollow. They might mean well, but not every message should be over-the-top excitement. That's <u>supposed</u> to be a good thing … but it's not because not everyone is in a place to receive it. A good sense of timing is critical in composing the right message.

Depressed extroverts are even worse. I know, because I was one. These people gripe and moan out loud. No one wants to hear it, but no one wants to "answer a fool according to their own folly" because he'll think himself wise (Proverbs 26:5). Their inner anxiety and energy feels like sludge, and as the old saying goes, misery loves company. They'd like nothing more than to drag you into their morass. Personally, I'd rather read the local obituary, and I regret all the times I let fly with my keyboard and made someone else's life unpleasant.

The point here is that one way or the other, our written content usually betrays us to some extent. By definition, it's only a representation of what we otherwise would say (or not say) with the voice. Sort of like how your social media presence is not <u>really</u> you. It is a reflection of you, or a representation of you. Even so, your messages can convey only so much of what you mean. Or, if you're the type to talk too much on social media, they'll over-convey something you *wouldn't* mean if your audience was physically present.

I avoid communicating in print when:
- I don't know the recipient well, or at all
- Either I or the recipient are in an emotionally volatile state
- The subject is a potentially inflammatory issue
- The recipient isn't familiar with my sense of humor
- It's an online forum where I barely know anybody
- The risk of needlessly offending someone looms large
- I have a comment that can easily be misinterpreted or taken out of context
- I can record a video message so people can properly receive it

More Growth from Awkward, Embarrassing Stories

There's nothing like the modern world of texts, emoticons, "ghosting" and e-mail to demonstrate the significance of written words. I prefer to highlight winning stories like Craig's connector message. But this next story is timeless, now reaching into the third version of my book. It includes some "ghosting," before ghosting was a thing.

I began my insurance years working for a very high-producing agent. We were the top-grossing agency in the state of Washington, and regularly ranked among the top ten nationwide, for that particular carrier. On the plus side, the agency owner was gifted with systems and processes. He had the entire sales strategy spelled out, start to finish. That made it a very learnable, repeatable process.

The downside was the stress level of working there. Many brand-name insurance offices have it. Anyone who wants to succeed as an owner must have a lot of drive. They need to instill that drive in everyone who works for them. There are several ways you can do this, but most of them eventually "drive" people away. Such was the case in this office. My employer's strategy for motivation was micro-management. To the degree I was compensated, it ended up being a losing deal.

Long before I resigned, however, came a key moment in communicating.

The sales staff took turns working Saturday mornings. We'd hammer the phones and try to set extra appointments. Even though he wasn't in the office, the agency owner would send e-mails to monitor progress. I never felt I could offer a satisfactory reply. So I'd answer these messages with a simple "Ok," signaling compliance with demands but not providing details.

This was my version of "ghosting," even though I did at least reply. I wasn't sure what I should say because I knew I'd get a terse reply one way or the other. Young people of all stripes now do this routinely. They receive a message online or via text, and the temptation is to not respond. If someone asks you later, you can tell them, "I saw it, but I was busy." Many times, that's somewhat true, but if the message concerned an awkward topic, it's easy to lie. I know I've feigned busy-ness a few times, to avoid taking ownership of my fear.

After a few rounds of this cat-and-mouse communication game, my troubles expanded. The boss became upset that I only replied "Ok." He wrote another intense message to say so. On the spur of the moment, I grabbed a scratch notepad on my desk and began to record call volume with tick marks. The next time he wrote to check on me, I replied: "50 phone calls, 10 connections, seven rejections, two possibles and one appointment set."

We never again had trouble communicating on Saturdays. He replied, "Keep at it, you'll find something eventually." I'd learned to adjust my message to the recipient. It was a "just the facts" conversation with a driven, Type-A personality. Most people reading this story side with me, resenting such a level of micro-management. But for me, it illustrates how I failed to employ a cardinal rule I already knew from being a communication major —Know your audience.

In this case, the "audience" was my employer. I should have known he'd want concrete details and numbers to satisfy his itch for progress. Especially after two or three months on the job. But this story happened much later, closer to eight or nine months after I started.

I should have known not to just reply "Ok." It took a few rounds of confrontation before I finally recognized the problem and changed my response.

Because of experiences like this, I send far fewer messages via text or e-mail than I used to. Especially in the early stages of a relationship. Even good messages that "should" make someone smile ... use them sparingly. We don't like to communicate into a void, getting nothing back, especially when we're being sincere. So when I <u>do</u> communicate in print, I take pains to decide whether or not to send the message at all.

When I <u>Do</u> Communicate in Print

I met copywriting master Joe LoGalbo through Vince Del Monte's mastermind. He was Vince's deputy coach for all things copy. As one of the group benefits, I got to schedule coaching calls with him.

Joe taught me the importance of creating "checklists" for writing. Having these at your desk makes it more difficult to write poorly, or incompletely. To the average reader, sales copy looks and sounds like informal language. You wouldn't necessarily think it has a "structure." But you'd be gravely mistaken.

The most important question Joe taught me to ask is, "What's the conversation the reader is already having in their head?"

Sales copy forces you to understand human psychology, specifically, the way your audience thinks. Are they likely to open your e-mail? Do they even *prefer* to get messages from you via e-mail? Do they respond if you write, or would it be better to send a video message? And those are just the basics. Then you must consider the timing, tone, urgency of and various audience segment responses to your message.

You might read this and think, "Edwards is trying to persuade me to pursue a career writing ad copy." Well, I certainly wouldn't discourage it. Done right, it's an extremely rewarding and interesting career. But I'm only trying to get you to *think like a copywriter* when you craft a message. Your messages should be ignored by fewer people.

Nowadays, you need to "catch" your audience at the time and place they'll respond to your message. You must forsake everything else in the name of the Journalist's Five W's – who, what, where, when, and why.

"Who" is the simplest part – make the message about "<u>you</u>" (as in, the audience) and you have their attention. Write about yourself, Aunt Sally, or Uncle Bob or anyone else you don't *know* the audience cares about and you're wasting time and space. You can go ahead and assume they don't care.

Dan Lok pointed out it's also important to be specific about who "you" is. He had a brilliant illustration: If you're walking down a busy street in a crowded city and you see someone you know, you have a better chance of getting their attention if you call them out by name. If you just holler, "Hey you!" in the middle of Times Square … you can imagine how it will turn out. (Except,

I suppose, over the last few months of the Coronavirus. But I digress.)

"What" signifies the solution, answer, satisfaction or feeling the audience seeks. If you're going to communicate in print, you need to know <u>what</u> your audience wants to talk about. Don't go straight for their aspirations. Most of the time, they're trying to solve a problem or overcome a challenge. Start from the place of where they *are*. My friend Ted Kallman, author of "The Nehemiah Effect," borrowed an illustration from evangelism:

"If you adhere to the idea of there being an absolute Truth (as we do), you still need to manage people at an individual level and from their perspective of 'truth' (understand and meet them where they are, not necessarily where they should be by your definition)."

That brings us to Where, which for all its simplicity is a forgotten part of effective writing. <u>Where</u> do they go to get more information? <u>Where</u> can they sign up? <u>Where</u> is the meeting to be held? <u>Where</u> can they see an example of this? I deleted hundreds of my early posts trying to get people to act because there was no "where."

If you think "where" suffers from neglect, you'll be shocked to discover how little attention gets paid to When. There's still enough good sense out there to tell people, "Order today!" or "Available right now!" That's the "white noise" aspect of "when." On social media we can even do live video and lock in orders in real time, just like a telethon. These, however, obscure subtler meanings of "when."

I refer to *frequency* when I talk about "when" — the question of "How frequently should I communicate with my audience?" There's a natural subjective side to this. Some audiences are hungrier than others, and some products are more interesting the more times you hear about them. But let's make a few general observations, in light of the kind of character we're pursuing.

Barraging people with nonstop e-mails, texts, instant messages, etcetera, will brand you as *something*. It may not be the identity you *want*. Particularly if it becomes "The Brand Everyone Ignores." I won't name any names here, but a certain TV provider called me at least once a week for an entire year after I canceled my subscription. They were certainly consistent; they were also consistently wrong. They are now so far out of my consciousness that I didn't think of this example until the third round of edits to the book.

Writing for the sake of "staying on people's radar" can also be hollow. It sometimes works, but there's only so much to talk about before people figure out you're just taking up their time. That's something you can do if you've achieved a position of prominence. Russell Brunson can do it to his audience, but that doesn't mean *my* audience will hear the same thing if I imitate him. Again, you will brand yourself as *something*. It may not be the identity you *want*.

On the other hand, you could be waiting a long time if you *never* write unless you have something earth-shaking to say. Let's assume that your others ducks are lined up; you have polarized and authentically acquired a list of followers who mostly resemble your client avatar. I'll use my list as an example: faith-based influencers, thought leaders and executives who thrive on connection, influence and publicity.

If you have five or six key ingredients to your formula, such as I write about in this book, then you can create content strategically linked to those ingredients. (*Shameless self-plug here:* Hiring a content ghostwriter can "fill in the gaps" for you on this. The more consistent your content, the more your "themes" emerge ... from which you can create "pillar chapters" of a book you can dictate through interviews and then have written for you.)

Once you have those pillars, you can begin filtering podcast guests, blog topics and messaging according to them. You'll also attract and encounter people, products and programs that correspond strategically to them. Just a short time ago, I got acquainted with Nick Pavlidis, a much more established and successful ghostwriter. He was due to release a course on how to become a ghostwriter just as the Coronavirus hit.

It was perfect for e-mail: a free webinar for an affordable course from a high-ranking competitor, about a service most of them are likely to want, and some might be likely to want to learn to do. Some might sign up and even become clients of Nick rather than me. Others might sign up, but not follow through. They might hire Nick, or they might not be able to afford him, so perhaps they could afford my services. Still others might not even know that ghostwriting is a service, much less want to learn how to do it. In every outcome, I win, directly or indirectly.

Would you agree with this criteria for when to communicate? If so, you're thinking like a Radically Generous Entrepreneur. As professionals, we need to remember there is at least more than one brain, one heart, and one soul involved in communication. It's our job to relate to our readers, seeing things from other viewpoints and attempting to meet them where they are, rather than where we think they should be.

As there's no use in being an expert lawyer ignorant of the spirit of the law, so is the idea of being an excellent grammarian and a terrible communicator. I'd rather work with a bad speller who knows what his audience wants to read than an excellent one who doesn't. I've read many messages and thought, "Well, there's a few minutes of my life I can never get back."

Here's the checklist I use for written communication:

- *Who* are you addressing? What are their demographics, commonalities?
- What are their *frustrations and fears*?
- What are their *wants and aspirations*?
- Is what you write *entertaining* as well as educating?
- Is what you write *personalized*? Do you invite the reader into your world, if only briefly?
- Will you take time to *read this aloud* to yourself? How does it sound when you read it?

This Is How We Do It

Joe LoGalbo also taught me the importance of creating memorable "mechanisms." These help audiences perceive your ability to lead in an organized manner.

On the sales page of my original book, "10 Secrets to Networking Success," we used an example of this. Specifically, I used the acronym "R.O.N" (Return on Networking) to help people visualize a system. Cameron Hall uses "P-F-C-Every-3," which stands for "Proteins, Fats and Carbohydrates Every Three Meals." Dr. Andy Garrett created the "V.I.C.E" system to describe the four corners of his Authentic Growth Blueprint: Values, Intrinsic Motivations, Character Strengths and Execution. These are simple enough to imagine, yet they imply sophistication and high-level knowledge on a subject.

Professionals engaged in any form of writing should make use of mechanisms to help people grasp the brand difference. You've already experienced this, though you may not have given it much thought. Have you ever received a free pizza from Domino's because it took more than 30 minutes to get to your door? You responded to their mechanism – "Delivered fresh to your door in 30 minutes or less."

Have you had a hamburger "Your way, right away," or rented a car because they said, "We'll pick you up"? Burger King and Enterprise Rent-A-Car have mechanisms, too. It's their way of saying, "This is *how* we do what we do, differently."

You can't always have a mechanism, especially in ongoing correspondence. But they're useful when crafting a message where you have an <u>intended outcome</u>. When you want people to purchase a product, think a certain way, make informed judgments about things or take "next steps," mechanisms are essential.

Calls to Action

Joe told me, "Depending on the length of the message, you want to include at least two or more calls to action. Be <u>very</u> specific about what you want them to do. Don't ask them to do four or five things at once. Just one task at a time."

Remember, I'm not trying to steer you toward becoming a writer on my team. We're talking about transferable habits that will get you better results on average, *anywhere you use them*. Whatever kind of message we send, we seek a positive <u>response</u> from the recipient.

Joe also believes persuasive messages give recipients "homework." It might be something as simple as opting-in for an e-mail list, subscribing to a podcast or answering "Yes or No" in a poll. If the object of the message is to get a response, a wordy memo of your thoughts without a specific call to action won't suffice. Remember the importance of "baby steps" in the size of action you ask them to take.

For example, don't say, "Click the link below, then subscribe, then like, then leave a comment and then check out the description box on my latest YouTube video."

Break those actions into bite-size amounts. Your audience follows one step, then another, and then another.

When "No" Doesn't Have to Mean "No"

Jayson Gaignard said the same thing about e-mail. If you must use it, break up messages for busy professionals in balance with all their responsibilities. If you do this, you can sometimes even get a "no" response to your request, but still convert it into a "yes."

Let's say you're trying to nail down an interview, like I do. This is where you can use the Journalist's Five W's <u>and</u> bite-size pieces. You don't want to be so vague that the recipient deletes the message. Jason Feifer, editor of Entrepreneur magazine, once posted a photo of an e-mail that did this the wrong way. The text read: "Dear Jason, I'd like to write articles for you. Who do I speak to?" That was it.

Jason disparaged this kind of message. It's almost a verbatim copy of what he receives from hundreds of people every day. How is he supposed to make decisions?

You want the reader to get enough detail to pique their interest. At the same time, you want to guide them through layers of detail – to qualify them, rather like a sales prospect. If I were trying to interview Jason, it might look something like this:

Dear Jason,

I listened to your recent podcast episode about novels. It was hilarious, entertaining, and informative.

I think the angle of "Pessimists' Archive" is a fantas-
tic way of sharing your thoughts with your audience.
(Remember, with influencers, tell them how much their
work means to you.)

I would love for my podcast audience of entrepre-
neurs to hear how your mind works. Would you be open
to a 30-minute Zoom or Skype interview?

Sincerely,
Paul Edwards

Do you see how little <u>thinking</u> Jason needs to do
when he reads this? The first paragraph lets him know
his hard work is paying off. Someone's listening, and
they appreciate what he says. He's making his point
well. Bravo. Influencers at every level love to hear that
their content is resonating and people get results from it.

The second paragraph respects Jason's time: "Here's
an opening for you to form a bond with more of your
target audience. You don't need to leave your office,
come up with questions, arrange for engineers or anything. All you need to do is show up and talk. Interested?"

At this point we've covered "who," "what", "where"
and some of "why." The only remaining details are
"when" and the subtler details of "why." Jason may ask
those in follow-up conversations, but we can omit them
from this message because he hasn't yet agreed in principle. Now, if Jason replies to this and says, "Yes," I can
proceed to discuss "when." If he replies with "No," I can
respond, "No worries. Out of curiosity, though … under

what circumstances would you say 'yes'?" This switches the direction of the exchange to "why."

Still, let's be honest and say it might not do any good. Perhaps the head of an operation like Entrepreneur simply doesn't do interviews, to avoid a deluge of requests for them. He might not be hungry for publicity.

But suppose I sent this same message to someone just starting a business publication. Suppose I sent it to someone rising through the ranks, who needs as many interviews as they can get? Remember the "farm team" principle, from networking with dream connections? It's the same concept. You should plan on doing 90 percent of your generous offers with people who are on the climb. Do enough of it over a long period of time, and you might flip that into doing it for people who occupy the summit.

In fact, that's just what I did. Vince Del Monte's mastermind group scheduled their May 2019 meetup in Vancouver, British Columbia. It's a half-day's drive from my house. With some caution, I began reaching out to some connections in the group, one by one:

Message 1
"Hey ... are you coming to Vancouver in May?"
"Yes, I'll be there."
Message 2
"I'm thinking of setting up a mastermind dinner. Interested?"
"Absolutely!"

<u>Message 3</u>
"Great! I'll keep you posted."

That's it. Do you see how it works? Bite-sized pieces, little by little. Not too much to think about. Questions where you most likely already know the answer. Busy entrepreneurs can answer questions like these in their spare moments. But when you "overdo it" with your messages ... well, let's try putting that all back into one paragraph:

"Hey, are you coming to Vancouver in May? I'm thinking of setting up a mastermind dinner and want to see if you're interested. Let me know and I'll keep you posted."

You may read this and think, "That's not too big of a bite to swallow." Let me tell you categorically — _nobody_ responded when I sent it all at once. Why does it work when you send it in pieces, versus just one message? Didn't we begin this chapter with an e-mail that turns results, despite being far more than five sentences?

You're correct, but remember, here we're concerned with figuring out how to hear "yes" more often. It may not come from the major influencer you're looking for. But you can always switch over to the farm team, provided you're willing to respect the same kind of cadence when it comes to what you put in print for them to see. All of this is useful to better understand the level of credibility or clout you have with your audience and the marketplace. In turn, you'll exercise far better discretion on what goes in your outbox.

And trust me … those major influencers will notice when they're dealing with someone who is Persuasive in Print.

CHAPTER 7 -
The Curator

Focusing on the Outcome

I remember the years I began to fully detach from network television. It was the late 1990s and the turn of the millennium. I recall the explosion in popularity of reality TV programming. It held zero interest for me; to this day, it's failed to fully capture my attention.

We all agree that something big shifted when the 21st century clicked into view. But you could probably find millions of opinions as to what exactly it was. If you ask me, reality TV signaled a process that's since gone viral in society. It has good and bad consequences. I think the good ones outweigh the bad. The process I'm referring to is called *democratization*.

Reality TV was born partially out of a Hollywood union squabble, if memory serves. Actors' trade unions went on strike, forcing studios to produce unconventional content. The big hit, as we fully departed the 20th century and moved into 2001, was the show *Survivor*. All of a sudden, second-rate actors who normally couldn't get a job were winning the ratings war. A lot more people began to have access to the entertainment industry. It had been "democratized."

At the same time, the internet was busy deconstructing several other guilded industries. Napster was sending shockwaves through the music establishment. Online news sources were tearing down the mighty oligopolies of cable and broadcast networks. A few years passed, and online options like Netflix emerged to wipe out video rental stores. Portable music devices that played MP3s eradicated the traditional record/cassette/CD store, and terrestrial radio. Online retailers, specifically Amazon, began to shutter traditional establishments like Sears, K-Mart and Toys R Us.

Whether you remember much of this or grew up after it, we've lived through a time that "democratizes" the best of what capitalist societies have to offer, like no other time in history. Just consider the last 20 years, in comparison with the previous 200, and the preceding 5,000. Truly, we live in times that our ancestors simply couldn't conceive, and I enjoy every minute of it.

The Democratized World

With this unleashing of freedom and enterprise comes a new problem for business. The barrier to entry for many industries dropped significantly. The Information Age found so many ways to deliver knowledge that it's hacking down the vaunted monolith of higher education itself. The days are already upon us that people with valuable skills waste precious resources pursuing pieces of paper nobody cares about. (My bachelor's degree in Communications hangs neatly on my wall. Nobody asks to see it in hiring me as a professional writer.)

This sets up a bittersweet reality. We can very easily acquire a new skill, and go into business in many different fields. But when we get there, we face a *very* difficult task: <u>making our marketplace aware that we exist</u>. It's not easily done when the market can choose someone in the Third World with a reliable internet connection. They can get the same work done for a fraction of your fee.

I Love Technology, But ...

This has powerful results, on the positive side. I interviewed Safwan Shah, CEO of PayActiv. Through a very simple application that costs employers nothing, companies like PayActiv have ended the paycheck-to-paycheck crisis for millions of American workers. They can now access their pay the same day they work to earn it. That is, to an orthodox Christian, unquestionably good news in perfect alignment with what the Word of God commands.

Famished for the home cooking of her native India one day, Poonam Vasantha Kumar went into business creating the next level of UberEats. Her New York-based app, Saavor, is launching a service to connect home-based chefs with hungry neighbors craving certain styles of cooking. New Yorkers will soon be able to order any number of delicacies _from their neighbors_. They'll be delivered by rideshare-style drivers. At the tap of a few buttons. Good relationships develop over shared meals, even if they start with a business transaction.

Bold Penguin CEO Ilya Bodner appeared on my show to share how his company is even bringing the insurance industry up to date with the times. Agents selling commercial policies can now submit one simple application and receive quotes from multiple companies in moments flat. It used to take me a good 30-60 minutes to run quotes through the ringer. If we can add speed to quoting, perhaps soon we can add speed to claims and underwriting decisions.

However, as these brave new legends of our economic expansion work away, a shadow stalks our basic humanity. The tidal wave of information and connection we have to what's going on around the world. The speed at which we're expected to move, like that of a smartphone. The comparison syndrome generated by visibility into millions of lives. The occupations displaced by technology, and the question of how to help the poor souls who lack skills to evolve.

All this leads to demand for the final overarching quality of the Radically Generous Entrepreneur: The Curator.

Webster's Dictionary defines a curator as "a keeper or custodian of a museum or other collection," or "a person who selects acts to perform at a musical festival." I chose this term to describe how to be intentional and defined about the people you want in your circles and the messages you send. You need to think about the venue, context and ambience of circumstances for meeting your target connections. You also should think about how you communicate once you've made contact with them.

An Inch Wide, A Mile Deep: Curating Your Signal Beacon

First, this ethos wormed its way into marketing. Data-driven analytics changed the game. You could actually see if people responded to your marketing or not. These days, you dare not attempt marketing without having a few key client avatars, certainly not in the online game, anyway. For entrepreneurs, this eliminated the need to say "yes" to anyone willing to pay for what they offered. They could now "choose" who they wanted as clients.

It was only a matter of time before this "targeted" approach permeated its way into other things. Business networking was not immune.

As I watched standard networking fade, I had difficulty naming its failure. Persisting with naming conventions like "networking group" was one reason. Nobody wanted to go hang out in a room full of salespeople and marketers. It was "old hat." I'm fond of saying that *concepts and ideas* have reached full maturity and ripeness when they become *products and labels*. That's what happened to traditional networking in the last decade.

Another unattractive quality of networking is its short shelf life. The same old people, having the same old conversations, following the same old routine. I've been in many groups that never exceeded more than 10 members. There wasn't any logic in going back. One group I knew dwindled to no more than five people meeting for lunch every week. The <u>same</u> five people!

As it should be, given the circumstances. Networking can no longer survive on the "shotgun" approach. You can't just "get out there and meet people." It's more complicated, and requires some advanced thinking. You can waste an awful lot of time schmoozing people who have no interest in you beyond being polite. You may as well mathematically increase the odds that you're in a room full of potential buyers. If you're a Radically Generous Entrepreneur, you want to be in a room full of amazing business leaders.

The other shortage in networking is, unfortunately, personal. Business is a great discussion topic. But in groups where personal life is "off limits," we effectively rule out significant dimensions of human existence. I can walk into a regular group and say something vacant like "Business is going okay, could be better." Or I can walk into my mastermind group and say, "I'm stuck and beating myself up because I can't grow my business. I'm getting angry at my family as a result." Which one is more gripping?

Podcasting and masterminds paved the way for me to leap over these hurdles. During the last two years, I conducted over a hundred interviews. My guests were coaches, consultants, influencers, authors, speakers, executives and civic leaders. I learned so much from these conversations that when I came to write for Aaron Walker, I had an encyclopedia in my head. I could draw on tons of stories, principles, examples and memorable illustrations from my guests. We also discussed deeply personal stories and topics. Many of my guests were influencers who'd overcome tremendous personal struggles.

You simply can't curate an old-fashioned networking group. Chamber of Commerce forums, Rotary clubs and the like usually have plenty of good people. At best, in my experience, they serve as "launching pads" for relationships. You can definitely meet good people there. But word will spread quickly if you start turning people away, and if your group is by invitation only, it won't be long before somebody you don't particularly want in it will demand to know why they've not been invited. If you knew of a location frequented mainly by your target clientele, it would make a better place to spend your time.

Better still: a location frequented by a target clientele of spiritual allies who cheer your success and help you overcome failure without judgment. How would that compare to casual yucks, wearing masks, with "familiar strangers" at your local Chamber gathering?

Suffice it to say, you'll need to be crystal clear on who you serve, and why you serve them. Armed with this, however, you can begin to network very effectively. As was the case for me, you can often do this without leaving your home. It's another way the tech revolution has "democratized" our access to one another. If your home city isn't populated heavily with the kind of people you want to meet, you can find them online!

My friend Matt Johnson (whom I met online, through podcasting) built a successful podcast management agency in San Diego called Pursuing Results. He's due to release a book called "Micro Famous," which captures perfectly what we should pursue as Radically Generous Entrepreneurs. Let the Kardashians and the Dwayne Johnsons of the world have their millions of followers. You worry about the small tribe that follows you.

Be famous, as Matt argues, to the *right* people. The ones who know you and appreciate your work. Carefully select them by being as specific and granular as you can. Then, you conduct a sustained campaign of over-delivering to them. This is how to curate your network.

How to Define Your Avatar

This is risky. I should charge for it, but I got it for free from a Radically Generous Entrepreneur. A giver. Freely I have received; I freely give.

This may not work for everyone, but I spent about 15 months fumbling about for my client avatar. I simply didn't know how to define them. So I would slap together some vague concept like "entrepreneur, business owner, marketer or sales professional." It was all fine and dandy, except I didn't know *why* I wanted to serve that community. You can't just say, "Because they have money."

I had to answer some hard questions … ones that require more than a passing thought. Why do I prefer to hang around other business owners? What is the context of our conversation? What do we usually have in common? Why do I prefer the company of business professionals over bureaucrats or academics?

The answers varied, of course, but the overarching theme goes back to business being a *spiritual* activity. With my fellow entrepreneurs, we can often take turns finishing each other's sentences, even if we're not in the same line of work. There's common experience, a mutual understanding of what creates value in others' lives. Entrepreneurs often become friends outside of business because they can attack life's difficulties on multiple fronts. Such is the case with my allies like Dave Culbreath, Femi Doyle-Marshall, Cameron Hall and Patrick Antonucci. We're not simply fellow businessmen; we're allies and friends.

Understanding this, I can list reasons *why* I prefer to network with entrepreneurs. I speak the same lingo, I know similar people, I have similar dreams. I respond to scenarios with a kindred spirit and attitude. I sense much more obligation and affection for my fellow man than your average bureaucrat; I'm not just here to stamp documents. I am far less concerned with ethical/ideological purity according to a particular cause than some nonprofit workers might be.

That's part one of nailing your avatar: knowing your *why*. The other part is "sketching" the ideal client, ruling out conflicting profiles, and solidifying the qualities of the right person.

I would lead with understanding people psychographically. If lifestyles and behaviors originate in the heart and mind, that's a better starting point. For example, I target faith-based people who exhibit a robust curiosity. Their pace is very deliberate, relaxed and confident. They are seldom in a hurry, even though they keep a tight schedule. They are generous and thoughtful themselves.

That turned out to be a little vague. Plenty of people in every avenue of life could identify with those qualities. But after landing my first writing clients, I figured out what I'd been missing: Demographics!

Politicians are known for doing this in reverse. That's one reason I believe voter turnout is low and apathy kicks in. If you want a majority of people in most Western societies to respond, you should begin with psychographics. I sigh when I hear politicians and journalists begin to talk about "the female vote" or "xyz minority group vote." I don't pretend to know the business side of politics, but courting currency from any group of human beings, whether it's money or votes, should begin with their spiritual identity.

Today, I target faith-based, usually married, mostly male online executives, thought leaders, coaches/consultants and influencers. They are too busy to form and execute their own content strategy. They need their voice "captured" by someone who possesses the wit of a mimic and the skill of a wordsmith. In the longer view, they need to build a content "tower," usually in the form of a book, based on their accumulated expertise and wisdom. That's where I fill the gap.

Once you know this, you can stop looking for networking opportunities in the wrong places. You can ignore the vanity fair because you know you won't find what you're looking for if you go inside.

Curating Yourself: An Analogy from Instagram

Another important facet of being a Curator is … curating yourself. You must understand what your audience is looking for so you can give it to them.

I met Luis Uribe as he pivoted away from fitness into media consulting for entrepreneurs in 2018. He'd grown fascinated with what makes content rise and fall on social media. Discovering, often by accident, why audiences respond, is a point of confusion for marketers. We talked about this in an interview he gave for Influencer Networking Secrets.

On Instagram, Luis advises clients to present "congruence" in their images and messages. "When I first meet clients, their Instagram feeds are all over the place," he said. "It's an assault on the human eye, and a very effective way of steering people *away* rather than *toward* your content."

One subtlety he mentioned is the preference for authentic video, juxtaposed with professional still shots on the profile. "Put a professionally produced video up there, and people will scroll right past it," he said. "You can save those for Instagram story and IGTV features. But put a video that looks raw and homemade, and IG users gobble it up."

Conversely, "authentic" still shots that lack a photographer's eye for composition, angle, background and lighting get short shrift. But beautifully produced, artistic photos with eye-catching composition still work magic.

Expressions of proportion, beauty, symmetry and congruence mixed with raw, real, vulnerable and homemade interactive moments. What does the popularity of these elements tell us about ourselves? How should it influence you as a Radically Generous Entrepreneur?

Human beings naturally seek equilibrium, symmetry, balance, order and beauty. Subconsciously, in our souls, these things communicate messages we desperately need to hear ... "All is well." "Everything will be fine." "Summer's coming." "Your Father is here."

So how do you present yourself, in person or online? Do you dress schlocky, trying to get away with minimum professional standards? (*I speak mainly to men here; ladies tend to do far better at this than we do*). Do you show up to social occasions unprepared, with nothing valuable to share? Would you be at all curious as to *how* people actually perceive your presence? I know we need to balance that against being obsessed with others' perceptions. But we should pay respect to our fellow human beings. If we bring a certain aura (or odor) into the room, there are things we can do to change that.

Meanwhile, raw and vulnerable conversations are powerful. We're aware of our individual emptiness, weakness, failure and folly. We need hope to move beyond it, and discussing these tendencies frankly brings reassurances: "You aren't alone." "Welcome to the club." "This has happened before, and it will happen again ... and it's going to be okay." "Been there, done that ... and I have a story to share."

You may read this and think, "Edwards! I'm not on Instagram. This doesn't apply to me. You're wasting my time." But I would argue that this applied long before Instagram existed. The social networks simply expose and verify through data what was already true. A thoughtful and detailed approach to self-presentation goes a long way if it's backed up by an equal commitment to authenticity.

Before Instagram was on anyone's radar, I recall coming of age in an era where *nobody* openly discussed their faults and failures. If you chose that path, it usually made you a pariah. It was okay to talk about handicaps and disadvantages, but you *never* showed your weakness. I'm glad those days are gone. You don't need to hide anymore, unless you're still convinced that everyone else has it together and you're the only one struggling. Just make sure you also look good while doing it.

Curating Your Intake

I mentioned masterminds at the outset because I'm a product of them. I chose the Iron Sharpens Iron mastermind, among other reasons, because I needed a place I could go to help me regulate my natural impulse toward entropy.

Barely one week into my membership, I found myself in the usual downward spiral of despair that things weren't working out. I hadn't yet launched my ghostwriting business, so it was another round in the crucible of trying to "prove" myself. The voice of my internal saboteur, "the flesh" as it's called in the Bible, was on a roll. I faced another losing round of persuading myself of my value to the marketplace.

I realized, however, that if I chose to shame and loathe myself, I would have to face a group of men who cared about me the next week. It would force me to choose between lying to their faces, trying to pretend I wasn't really there, or repenting and confessing my failures. To me, the best option was to admit my shortcomings quicker. It neutralized the power of the argumentative voice in my head because it's hard to accuse yourself of something you've already admitted to doing.

Moreover, technology being useful as it is, I found I could easily disclose this struggle to the men in my mastermind group for them to review at their convenience. I didn't even have to wait until Monday morning, when our group usually meets over Zoom. It wasn't long before I made the connection that masterminds built on personal and professional development, particularly from a Judeo-Christian ethic, make it more difficult to sin as frequently as in isolation.

I'd been looking for a company like the men of Iron Sharpens Iron for my entire life.

Curating the Audience

Now, let's talk more of curating the people outside your immediate social circle. Let's assume you've curated where you'll show up, among whom and how. We now want to turn to <u>whom</u> you'll attract when you appear. The people that respond will speak volumes about the energy you emit.

At church, I lead a group of young men in discipleship. They are an interesting bunch. Some are entrepreneurs, and others may one day become so. But I find myself asking God, "What has made them willing to raise their hand to join our group?" We have always been open and inviting, but not everyone accepts when I extend invitations.

Do you recall what I shared about polarity, when it comes to magnetism? One key to understanding is a theme I received in 2019, "A Tree in Due Season." Taken from Psalm One, I had multiple people tell me the same thing. Corey Blake, who appeared twice on my podcast that year, had this to say:

"<u>Paul is an oak tree</u>. Not many podcast hosts can hold the space for a deep interview the way that Paul can. He is profoundly present for his guests and allows the conversations to organically take shape in a way that

is intriguing to follow and unique in its unfolding. He is indeed a spiritual teacher with much to offer listeners. "

From this, I came to see that something in my personality drew people who are somewhat reserved or introverted. If you've ever found a special place in nature, like a big tree nestled at the bank of a river, you might start to get the picture. The young men often respond as though they've "fled" from predators in the wild, and found a quiet spot to sit down and rest. I'm intentional about creating a setting that allows for the human soul to express itself without judgment but nevertheless tells the truth and beckons the best from people.

So the majority of my audience is less and less mysterious, as time goes on. I have "curated" them, though not by insisting on membership cards or personality tests. I simply trust that there's far more at work in magnetism between people, and I don't try to force those I repel to like me. This doesn't mean you need to hire bouncers at your events, in case the wrong crowd shows up. This is about trusting in the way spiritual magnetism works, and paying attention to the most common results you get.

Individuals who respond to you won't usually be conscious of why they do, and their reasons won't be universally similar. But you'll find a majority coming toward you for common reasons. This gives me a mandate to write and express myself in a way that expounds on my character strengths and passions. I can trust from there that the message will find its way to the right people.

Curating Prospects and Clients

Curating your clientele takes time and practice. I wish I had more "science" on it, but I'm careful to apply that word to anything so difficult to measure or predict. I don't believe in a "science" to define and analyze the infinite variety of God expressed through human beings. The only defined measurement I keep on any human being is that of my own behavior. I can quantify and qualify my own actions; what everyone else thinks or does is far too complex.

The way I curate my clientele is mainly by sidelining traditional methods of acquiring them. That old process leaves far too many variables open. You might be in a different line of business where it isn't nearly so important. If you're simply selling t-shirts, then you have more of a responsibility of curating suppliers, distributors and employees. My hat's off to you, but this will still be valuable in your deliberations.

This book is about relationships. I'm only in business because of relationships. So why would I want to focus my primary marketing energy on *strangers*?!

When entrepreneurs like Aaron Walker, Andy Garrett, Luis Diaz or Bill Sturm recommend me to someone, there's a lot less selling to do. In fact, I've had no traditional "sales" conversations since I became a ghostwriter. There are simply exchanges between amazing people who know other amazing people. It isn't my practice to pursue business relationships with people I don't know, or who haven't been referred to me.

Even if you're marketing a product to strangers for 20 bucks, you're *delivering* that product using vendors and suppliers. Somewhere in that supply line, you'll be forced to choose between an impersonal partnership, or one based on a relationship. What is the price of convenience and expedited process worth to you? It might be just what the doctor ordered … or, it might not.

Oh, the pain this brought me in my days as an insurance agent! I was so desperate to prove myself as a competent salesperson. I was so frightened at the prospect of being fired for failure to sell. I lived under such anxiety and self-imposed hardship to *produce* when I could have simply focused on farming success from the powerful people who gathered around me!

Curating your prospects and clients implies getting very clear about who you serve, and why. Having said that, I want to add that it doesn't *automatically* mean you reject anyone and everyone who doesn't fit your ideal client profile.

One of my favorite clients to write for is Bill Sturm, executive vice president of operations for Rausch Sturm, LLP. They're a debt collection agency. Bill has a brilliant strategic concept — "copywritten debt collection letters"! He's certainly not moonlighting as an executive coach or marketing maven. But he thinks like a Radically Generous Entrepreneur. His firm is a national standard bearer for fair, humane and respectful conduct in a task no one really wants to do.

So always be open to curating people who don't

fit the avatar. You probably aren't aware of the kind of groups Bill's likely to belong to, but after a while I suddenly realized I knew several people who play at a similar level, and started by introducing him to Safwan Shah. It was only days later that Bill offered to recommend me to some of his best peers throughout his industry.

Curating Outcomes

One of the young men in the discipleship group I lead, Devon LeMaster, asked a very thoughtful question one night. He wanted to know where I saw our group going. Did I have some sort of grand agenda? Were we going to expand and start some kind of movement? I love young men's questions. They remind me of the free-spirited nature of being in your early twenties, open to far more possibilities than when you're older.

I couldn't answer Devon in the moment, but I have the answer now. A few days later Aaron Walker quoted his mentor on our mastermind call: "I only want to sink my teeth into things God is up to." It hit me like a ton of bricks. I have tried enough of my own schemes to know how they end up. No wonder God keeps telling us to wait on His timing.

In the meantime, however, I told Devon that there was one thing I would definitely do: Build relationships. Wherever this group is leading, even if it doesn't have much further to go, I will build relationships and add value to people. It's what I did best during 17 months of entrepreneurship with no income, and it's what I do best now. There simply isn't a better place to invest time, talent or treasure than in the people already surrounding you. They tend to do a lot of the heavy lifting when it comes to improving your life.

Even as much as you can't control outcomes, I think it's imminently possible to curate them. You can keep stacking meaningful connections, one on top of the other, until that Radically Generous Entrepreneur reveals himself or herself. At an intrinsic level, for the pure joy of helping others, you can go far beyond what the average person is willing to do. After that, it's just a matter of having a solid offer of a service or product the market actually wants.

"Edwards, you make it sound so simple," you may grumble under your breath. I understand that sentiment. I used to flounder about with relationships myself. Often, we have to come to the end of our own idiocy before we'll consider learning from people with more experience than we have. But remember: There is no simplistic solution like "Just study what Tony Robbins or Grant Cardone do and then imitate it." (I tried that too, and failed.)

Let's instead set out on the mission of becoming a Curator, and aligning our work, efforts, connections and experiences with who we are on the inside. If we cannot immediately get paid, then let's prepare until someone's willing to pay us.

LET'S WORK TOGETHER

I f you are a faith-based thought leader, influencer, coach/consultant or content-based online entrepreneur, I've had occasion to serve people like you joyfully in exchange for green certificates of appreciation that help me afford my supplement habit.

If you want to assemble a robust, multi-layered content library over time that can eventually take form in a bestselling book ... OR you already have it, but don't have time to write it ...

If you feel like you're missing opportunities to impact your world, change mindsets and attract more people into your following ...

If life, family and business keep you so intensely focused that you physically can't swing the amount of time needed to write and edit content …

If you'd like to "outsource your voice" and automate your outreach with authentic content tailored to your audience …

I am open to having a conversation.

Website: https://thepaulsedwards.com

Facebook, LinkedIn, Instagram and on Twitter @ thepaulsedwards

Thank you for reading. I appreciate your attention.

ABOUT THE AUTHOR

Bestselling author, podcast host and executive ghost-writer Paul Edwards wears many hats. He's a disciple of Christ, a husband, a father and a mentor to younger men in the faith. He's an amateur theologian, a men's physique competitor, a voice mimic and a recovering insurance salesman.

Paul is a first-generation, Spanish-speaking immigrant to the United States, with African heritage and

Middle East combat experience. He's lived in five different countries (Canada, US, UK, Germany and Iraq) and holds three passports.

Paul does two things well – words and people. If he's not writing content or books for clients, you'll find him creating introductions or opportunities for them. If that fails, he'll be in the gym.

On his podcast, also titled *Influencer Networking Secrets*, Paul interviews thought leaders, executives, entrepreneurs and influencers. Conversations take place at the border of the natural and supernatural, and cover business, technology, faith, athleticism, mindset and personal development.

As part of his first bestseller, *Business Beyond Business*, Paul created the aspirational avatar of the Radically Generous Entrepreneur.

Using qualities and principles distilled from years as a service-oriented marketer and personal brand builder, Paul discovered the secrets of how influencers network, and the secrets of networking with influencers.

With over 15 years of joy-filled marriage to Shannon and nearly a dozen years as father to Grant and Chase, Paul is a Kingdom-builder to young men of faith in the cities of Olympia, Lacey and Tumwater, Wash., where he has made his home since 2005.

CPSIA information can be obtained
at www.ICGtesting.com
Printed in the USA
JSHW030118170321
12579JS00001B/53